The Ashford Book of
New Zealand Folk Art

The Ashford Book of New Zealand Folk Art

Maryke Lups-Frowyn

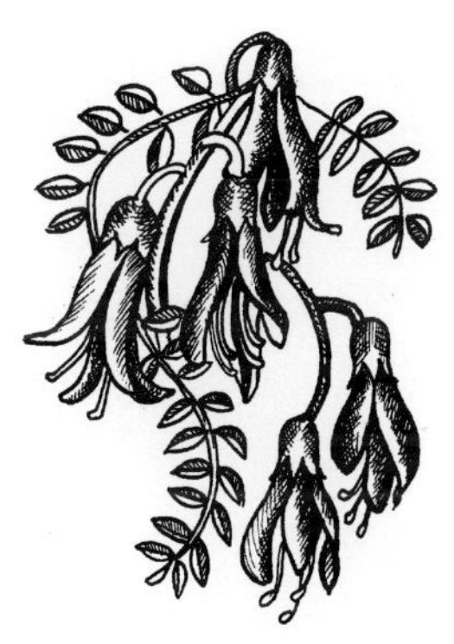

SHOAL BAY PRESS

First published in 1998 by
Shoal Bay Press Ltd
Box 17661, Christchurch 8

Copyright © 1998 Maryke Lups-Frowyn

ISBN 0 908704 47 x

Photographs: Jon Hunter
Incidental line drawings: Rachel Thornton

Printed by Rainbow Print Group, Christchurch

Contents

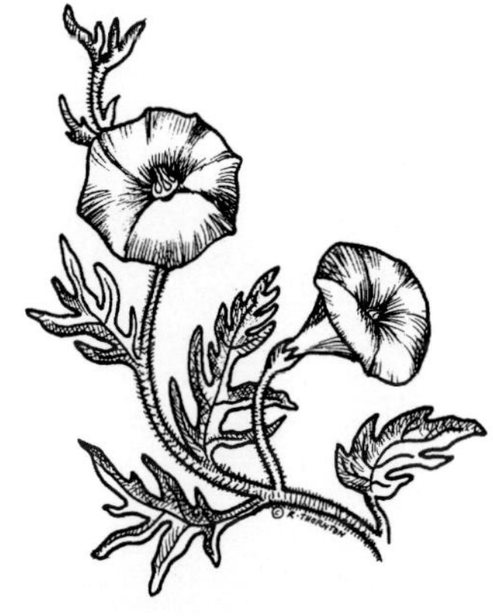

Acknowledgments

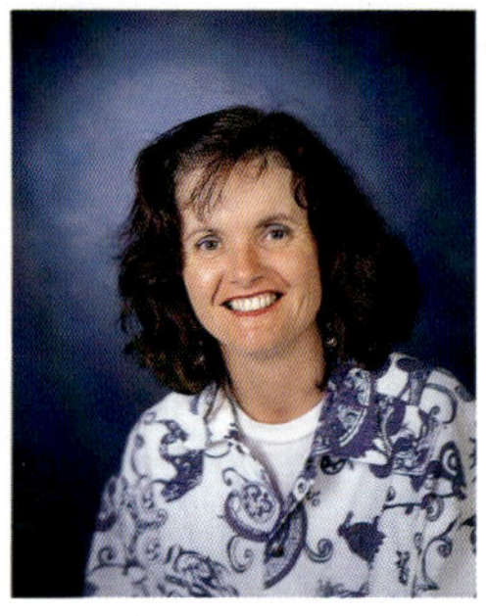

Maryke Lups-Frowyn

First of all I thank my family. My husband Henk, for putting up with all my hours of painting and for the lovely meals he cooked when I had, once again, no time – love you. Paul and Rachel, my two wonderful kids, whose mummy is always so busy – I will have more time to spend with you now.

Then all my students, especially the women from my Risingholme and Little River classes, for your encouragement and listening ears. We have really become friends over the years.

To Maurice Cook from Papanui High School and Raewyn Cooke, from Risingholme Community Centre, thank you for having faith in me when I started to teach, seven years ago, and for your support over the years.

My dear friends Joanne Webber and Ann Ohs I thank for all those shared thoughts, not only about painting, but life in every aspect.

Thanks to my special friends in Diamond Harbour: Anne van der Kooi and Annelies Geerts, for all the good talks and cups of coffee when I've needed a break.

To Barbara Corcoran, for her work on the class texts, and Diana Hosted, for her work on this book, thank you – it was a challenge putting my pigeon English into proper English!

Special thanks to David Elworthy from Shoal Bay Press, and Richard Ashford and Rowena Hart from Ashford Handicrafts Ltd for having faith in my ability to produce this book.

I also thank Jon Hunter for his beautiful photography, Rachel Thornton for her lovely decorative line drawings and Chroma Acrylics Pty Ltd in Australia for supplying Jo Sonja's paints and mediums used in this book.

Naturally, I thank the great painter and creator who gives all of us inspiration and creativity.

Maryke Lups-Frowyn

The Story of Ashford

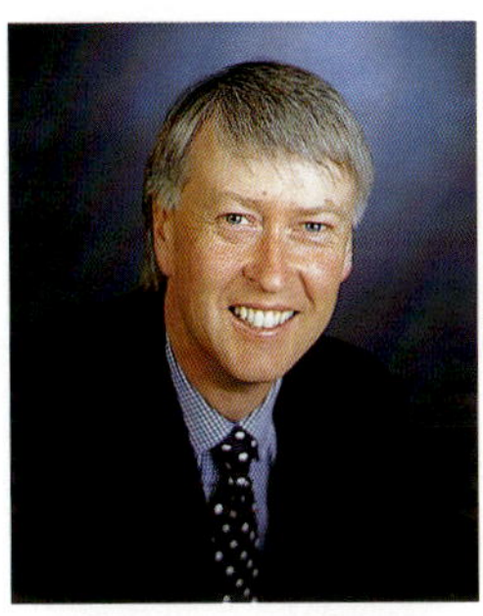

Richard Ashford

Since 1934, when Walter Ashford founded the company, Ashford Handicrafts has become a world leader in the manufacture of quality spinning wheels and weaving looms. Over 500,000 Ashford spinning wheels are currently used around the world.

Today Walter's son Richard Ashford manages the busy export company which is located at Ashburton, in the South Island of New Zealand.

In addition to its large range of spinning and weaving equipment Ashford manufactures a unique range of wooden toys, dollshouses and other craft items, all of which are available in kitset form unfinished. As Maryke demonstrates in this book, the natural beauty of all these products can be enhanced by the technique of folk art painting. Following her detailed instructions you too can use your own artistic skills to create an heirloom that your family will treasure forever. Maryke's easy-to-follow step-by-step plans will take you into a new world – the world of folk art painting.

Try your local craft store for folk art paints.

All the wooden pieces that are painted in this book are available from an Ashford distributor near you (see Appendix), or write to:

Ashford Handicrafts Ltd
PO Box 474
Ashburton, New Zealand
Fax: 64 3 308 8664

Or: E-mail us on sales@ashford.co.nz

Introduction

My introduction to folk art painting was in my home country, the Netherlands, in 1982. A friend of mine encouraged me to attend folk art painting classes as a form of relaxation from an intense work situation I was in at the time. Although I took some persuading, I know now that it was one of the best decisions I have ever made; I really fell in love with this art form. I learnt such a lot from my teacher who, using teaching manuals she had written, taught us step by step the traditional style of Bavarian and Dutch floral painting.

There was a big change in my life in 1983 when I emigrated to New Zealand with my husband and especially in those first years, when there were some quite lonely times, I found solace in keeping a link with home through my painting. At that time though, folk art was nearly unknown in New Zealand and I missed the contacts from Europe and the everyday folk art displays.

I felt the need to share my passion with others. So in 1991, after nearly eight years of painting on my own and sometimes selling my work through friends and retail outlets, I started to teach folk art. I began with two continuing education classes for adults. Nearly six years later the classes have grown from two to six a week.

Through my teaching at Ashfords, Ashburton, I met Richard Ashford and was given the opportunity of writing and painting a book on New Zealand folk art using Ashford's beautiful wooden products as the projects. So here it is: a New Zealand book on folk art. I hope you enjoy painting the projects. As well as using the Ashford's wood pieces you can also adapt the designs to your own items. Creativity has no boundaries!

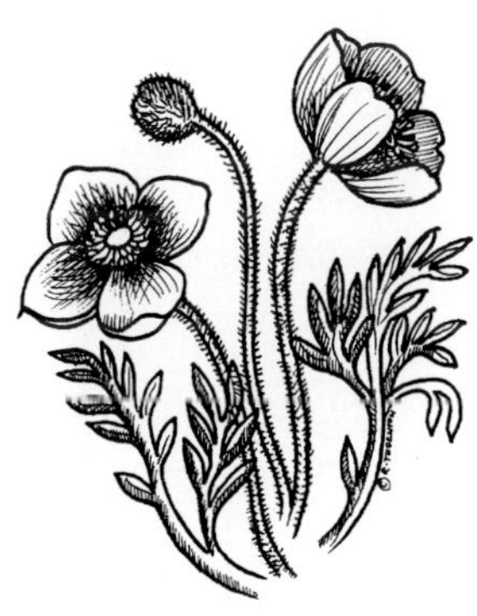

General Information

PREPARATION OF SURFACES

Most of the painted items in this book are made out of customwood (craftwood) or pine, but you can adapt the patterns to other surfaces as well, so I have included instructions for a few others.

Customwood or craftwood

The edges of customwood are mostly rough. A good method to get a smoother finish is to seal the edges first with Jo Sonja Tannin Blacker Sealer, let dry and then sand with fine sandpaper (400-1200 grit).

Basecoating is the next step. I use a No. 25 soft flat brush and basecoat in long even strokes.

When dry, sand the customwood again, especially the edges. Remove the dust with a tackcloth and basecoat again.

Two coats is usually enough, although some more transparent colours need three coats.

To get a smoother finish I mix my basecoat with Jo Sonja Clear Glazing Medium.

Pine

Most of the pine projects in this book are stained because I love the look of the timber and feel it is a shame to cover the beautiful grain under a coat of solid paint.

Waterbased staining

In an old saucer mix your colour with water in the proportion 1:5. You should have a watery mixture. With a lint-free cloth rub the mixture onto the wood following the woodgrain. (Test the colour first on the back of your project. Better to start too light.)

When dry, sand the wood with fine sandpaper, again following the woodgrain. If you find the colour too light, a second coat can be rubbed on and again sanded when dry. You should end up with a very smooth finish.

Seal the timber with a thin coat of Jo Sonja Clear Glazing Medium.

Metal (including steel, tin, brass, copper)

The piece should be washed in hot soapy water and cleaned well, using a brush with firm bristles.

After drying, rinse with a mixture of water and vinegar to remove any grease. Dry well.

Seal the metal with a rust preventative or metal primer, according to the manufacturer's instructions.

Basecoat with two or three coats of acrylic paint. Let dry between coats and sand very lightly with fine sandpaper.

Let the paint cure for a couple of days before decorating.

Terracotta

Terracotta is often a little dusty when bought, so clean the piece with a damp cloth and let it dry.

Seal with Jo Sonja Sealer inside and out if you want to paint directly onto the terracotta. When using paint to basecoat, mix a little Jo Sonja Sealer with it. Usually two coats are needed. Sand lightly between coats.

After decorating, finish the item with two coats of waterbased varnish.

With a garden pot, it is best to keep the plant in a plastic container and sit the plastic container inside the decorated pot.

Glass

Wash the piece in hot soapy water and let it dry. Rinse with a mixture of vinegar and water.

Seal the portions of glass you want to decorate with Jo Sonja Sealer or Jo Sonja Glass and Tile Medium. Follow the instructions on the bottle.

Soaps and candles

Apply a coat of Jo Sonja Sealer, then paint your design. Finish with a coat of waterbased varnish.

BASIC SUPPLIES

Paint

In this book I have used Jo Sonja artist's colours and mediums. These are available in many art and craft shops around New Zealand and overseas. I also use Matisse brand colour paints and Plaid Folk Art, and these will be mentioned with the specific project.

Jo Sonja Artist's Colours
Black: Carbon Black
Whites: Warm White, Smoked Pearl
Yellows: Yellow Oxide, Yellow Light, Raw Sienna
Reds: Burgundy, Napthol Crimson, Indian Red Oxide, Napthol Red Light
Blues: French Blue, Aqua, Sapphire, Cobalt Blue Hue, Colony Blue, Ultra Blue Deep
Greens: Pine Green, Green Oxide, Teal Green, Pthalo Green
Browns: Brown Earth, Fawn, Burnt Umber
Purples: Amethyst, Diox. Purple
Grey: Nimbus Grey
Golds: Rich Gold, Pale Gold
Orange: Norwegian Orange

Jo Sonja Background Colours
Red: Spice
Blues: Azure, Dolphin Blue
White: Soft White

Plaid Folk Art
Yellow: Primrose
Green: Napthol Southern Pine

Matisse
Green: Antique Green

Jo Sonja Mediums
Tannin Blocking Sealer for Wood
Flow Medium
Clear Glazing Medium
Decor Crackle Medium
Crackle Medium
Satin polyurethane varnish (water-based)
Satin polyurethane varnish (oil-based)
Texture Paste

Antiquing medium (Burnt Umber oil paint and artist's turpentine 1:4)

Brushes
There are various excellent brands of brushes on the market. I mostly use:
No. 0 or 1 short liner brush
No. 3 and No. 5 round synthetic or sable brush
No. 8 flat brush
3/8-inch angular brush
1/4-inch comb brush
1/4-inch deerfoot brush

For basecoating and varnishing I use 1-inch flat brushes (a different brush for each).

Please look after your brushes; they are the tools of the trade! Never leave them standing in water – that will only ruin them. Rinse them under the tap after painting and work some detergent into them. Rinse again.

Rub a little vaseline into the bristles of your round brushes and roll them back into a point. Protect the bristles by covering them with a section of plastic straw. If the bristles on your brushes do become damaged you will find they will straighten again if you stroke the brush against a warm lightbulb!

Wooden pieces
All wood pieces are manufactured by:
Ashford Handicrafts Ltd
PO Box 474
Ashburton
New Zealand
Tel: (64 03) 308-9087. Fax:(64 03) 308-0664

Ashford products are available from craft shops around the world. For the name of your nearest stockist, contact your national distributor.

Other equipment

Palette: I use a strip palette, which is excellent for blending purposes, and after each painting session I tear off the waxed palette paper and dispose of it. But it is fine to use an old dinner plate or a plastic tray instead. To make a damp palette, place dampened paper towels on your palette and lay a piece of baking paper or plastic clingwrap on top of them. This will prevent your paints from drying out too quickly.

Water jar
White chalk pencil (to free-hand designs onto your item)
Transfer paper (graphite paper, light and dark)
Magic tape (to hold your pattern to the piece while tracing it or for masking areas off)

Stylus (for tracing your design onto your item. Also useful for making nice round dots)
Sandpaper (40-1200 grit)
A soft eraser (for erasing transfer paper lines)
Sea sponge (for a sponged background)
Soft lint-free rags (for staining timber and drying your brushes)
Tackcloth (to remove dust after sanding your piece)

BASIC TECHNIQUES

Basecoating

Use a soft brush to apply an even coat of paint to achieve an opaque coverage on the piece you want to decorate.

Several thin coats are better than one thick, uneven coat. Usually two to three are needed with a light sanding in between.

Mix a little Jo Sonja Clear Glazing Medium with your paint for a nice smooth finish.

Floating

This is a technique for shading or highlighting and is done with a flat brush, preferably a wide flat No. 8.

Wet the brush and blot lightly on a damp sponge sitting in a saucer of water. This way, when you blot onto the sponge you have the right amount of water on your brush for floating.

Dip one corner of the brush into the paint and stroke the brush up and down on the palette until the colour is graduated – dark colour on one side, a medium tone in the centre and clear water on the other side.

Move to your project and place the side of the brush with the most paint onto the part to be shaded or highlighted.

Loading a round brush

Wet the brush and roll back into a point on your palette.

Pull through the paint, rolling the brush into a point while doing so. Load the brush nearly up to the ferrule (the metal part).

Top-loading a round brush

Fully load the brush with one colour. Scoop up a little of a darker or lighter shade of paint on the tip of your brush as if you were scooping up icecream and paint your stroke.

Most of the second colour will stay at the top of your stroke.

Double-loading a round brush

Fully load the brush with one colour. Sweep one side of your brush through a second colour. Now you have one side loaded with the first colour and the other with your second colour. When painting your stroke, hold the brush in such a manner that each side paints a different colour. The colours should not be blended when you paint your stroke.

Drybrushing

I sometimes use this technique instead of the floating technique for highlighting and shading. As the name implies, you must use a dry brush.

Pick up a little paint on a round No. 5 brush and then wipe it on a paper towel, flattening the bristles by fanning them out.

Lightly skim over the surface of your work with the tips of the brush – you should still be able to see the colour underneath.

Gradually build up the density of colour by applying several layers of paint.

Rake brushing

Mix a little water with your paint. Pick up paint on the tip of your rake brush and wipe some off on your palette.

Lightly rake off the paint in the direction you want it to go. Practise first on your palette.

(Note: With bears, rake the paint in the same direction as the pile of the fur.)

Stippling

Stippling is done by lightly bouncing a deerfoot brush, to give the effect of trees, hills, animal furs etc.

Use a dry brush and pick up some paint from your palette. Bounce the brush on paper towelling a couple of times before touching the piece.

Do not stipple too heavily – keep it light and airy, allowing the background colour to show through.

It is important to hold your brush at an angle

when stippling as otherwise this method takes its toll on your brushes.

Sponging

Dampen a sea sponge and squeeze out the excess water. Pick up some paint on the sponge and bounce the sponge onto paper towelling to take off the excess paint.

Lightly sponge onto the wood piece, not too heavily. Additional layers of colour can be sponged on top.

Line work

When using a liner brush always mix your paint to thin, inky consistency.

Load the brush with paint and roll back into a point. Hold the brush perpendicular when painting fine lines or scrolls, so the paint flows off the bristles more easily.

Balance the weight of your hand on your little finger.

Brush Strokes

I use most of the brush strokes well known in folk art and decorative painting techniques (see p.13).

Comma Stroke

Mostly done with a round brush No. 3 or No. 4.

Fully load the brush with paint and roll back into a point on your palette.

Rest your hand on the surface of your project. Hold the brush at a slight angle and touch the brush to the surface.

Press the bristles down to form the head of the comma. Slowly pull the brush and lift at the same time; allow the bristles to return to a point.

So: Press – pull – lift.

Teardrop

A teardrop is a straight comma stroke.

Load the brush with paint and press the bristles onto the surface. Instead of slightly curving the stroke, pull straight down. Lift the brush, ending with a fine point.

S Stroke

I often use this stroke for leaves.

Load the brush with paint. Roll back into a point

on your palette. Hold the brush in an upright position. Start with a fine line and slowly add pressure to form an S shape. Release the pressure.

Lift the brush from the surface, ending with a fine line.

U Stroke

This stroke is used in Dutch floral painting (Assendelfter painting) and I like to use it for my roses.

Load the brush with paint. Usually you will use two colours, with the lighter colour on the top of the brush. Touch the tip of the brush to the surface and pull a line.

Now add pressure and wiggle the brush lightly to curve into a U shape. Release the pressure and end with a line.

Special Effects

Crackling

This will give your project an aged look. There are two methods of doing this:

Method 1 (Jo Sonja Decor Crackle Medium)

In this method, which makes for bigger cracks, the Decor Crackle Medium is like the meat in the sandwich, i.e. it is applied between two layers of paint.

Paint the surface with one colour. Let dry.

Apply some Decor Crackle Medium. Leave until it is touch dry (20-30 minutes).

Using a soft brush, apply a contrasting colour, lighter or darker than the basecoat. Do not overstroke as this will lift off the Decor Crackle Medium.

Let dry. Sand lightly.

The crackling looks best when it is accentuated by antiquing medium being rubbed into the cracks.

Method 2 (Jo Sonja Crackle Medium)

This method creates larger numbers of very fine cracks, making the object look like crazed china.

Apply two or three heavy basecoats of a Jo Sonja artist's colour. Let dry.

Apply some Crackle Medium as soon as possible with a large soft brush. Do not overbrush.

Cracks will start to appear immediately but the medium keeps on working until completely dry.

With this method you can crackle certain areas

Brushstrokes

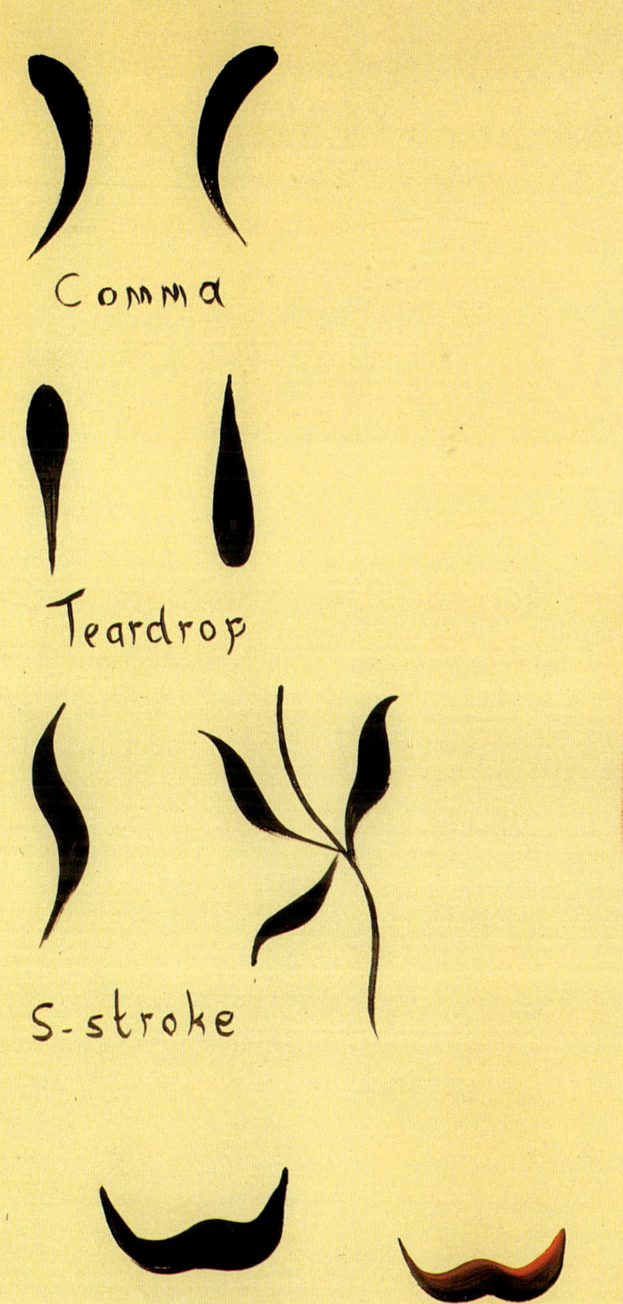

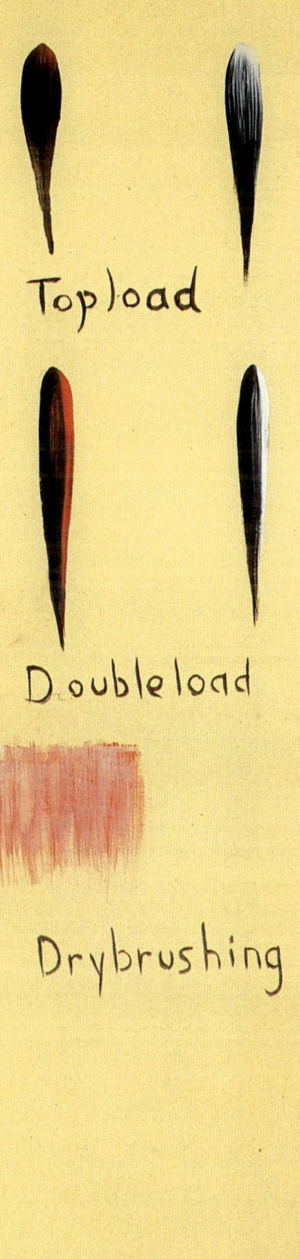

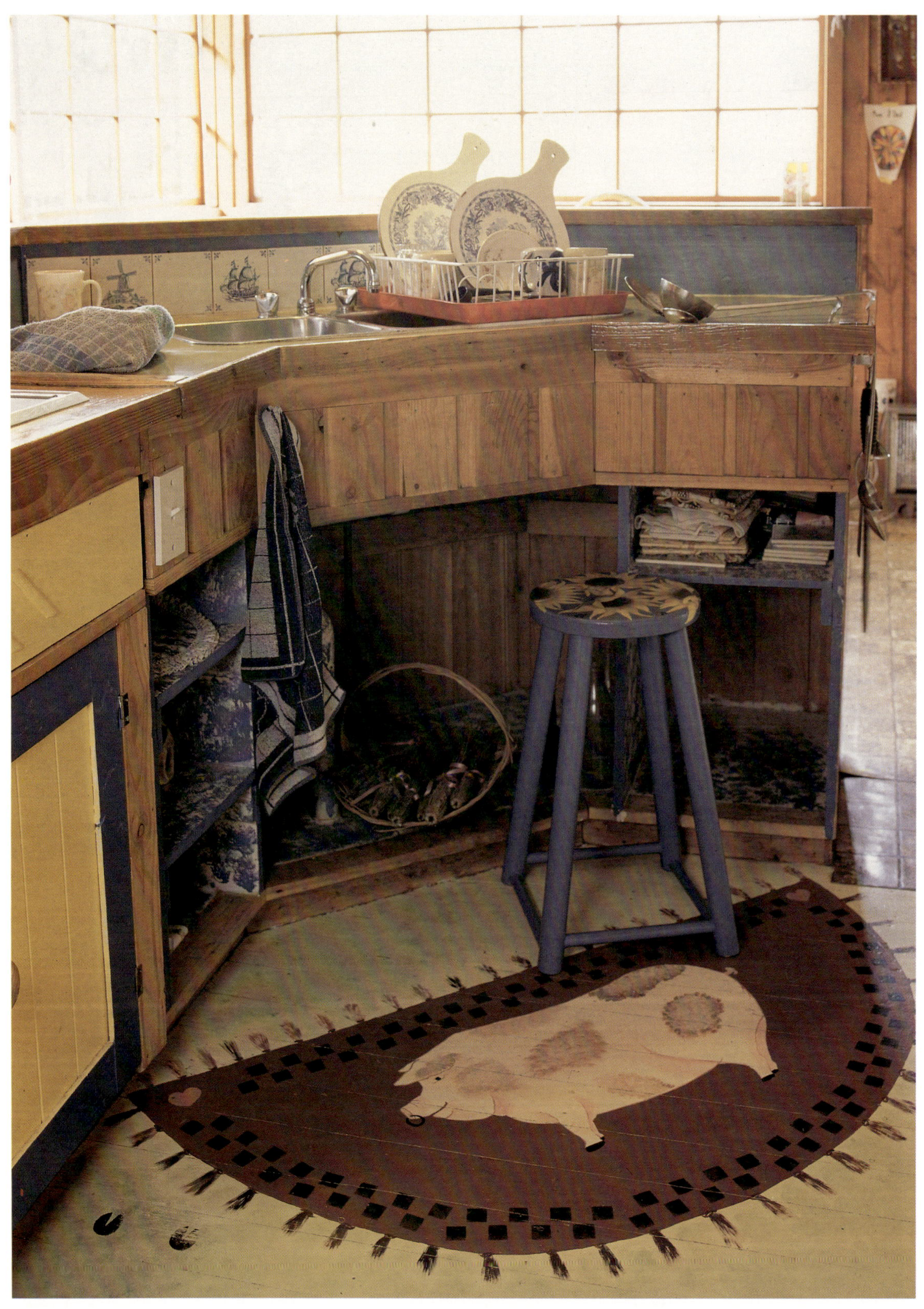

Our kitchen pig

of a painting, and then accentuate the crackling with antiquing medium rubbed into the cracks.

Try to do your crackling while the paint is still fresh, but if you don't have time, slip the painted project into a plastic bag and keep it in a cool place.

Antiquing

Antiquing your project after painting will give it a mellow look. I don't antique every project I paint as sometimes I like brighter colours, such as in the Dollshouse and the Teddy Bear Christmas Tree. But certain projects look better if they are mellowed, like the Cutlery Box and Tray.

As an antiquing medium I use artist's turpentine mixed with Burnt Umber oil paint 4:1 until it has a creamy consistency. Store this mixture in a small, glass, covered container.

Rub antiquing medium on in a circular motion, using a lint-free cloth and working towards the centre from the sides.

Sometimes I antique just where I want to deepen shading or divide areas, eg under flowers and leaves.

Use a mop brush to soften the antiquing so that it fades out into the painting.

Once you are happy with the results, let the project dry for a few days – sometimes it can take up to a week if the weather is cold.

Varnish with two or three coats of Jo Sonja satin polyurethane (oil-based) varnish.

If you are new at this and want better control of the antiquing process you can give your project one light coat of water-based varnish before antiquing. that way you can 'undo' any antiquing that doesn't work!

To avoid staining your hands wear disposable surgical gloves while you antique. Dispose of the used cloth carefully as it will be combustible.

Varnishing

For all the projects in the book I have used Jo Sonja satin polyurethane varnish, either water-based or oil-based.

Before varnishing, remove all your tracing lines with an eraser or a little artist's turpentine on a lint-free cloth. Remove any dust with a tackcloth.

Use a soft varnishing brush (keep one brush just for varnishing) and apply the varnish in long even strokes in one direction. Let dry.

Lightly sand with fine sandpaper. Remove the dust again with a tackcloth and varnish again with brushstrokes in the opposite direction. You will need two or three coats.

I usually let my projects dry in the bathroom – the steamy atmosphere, after I have run a hot shower for a few minutes, absorbs the dust – but keep the door closed!

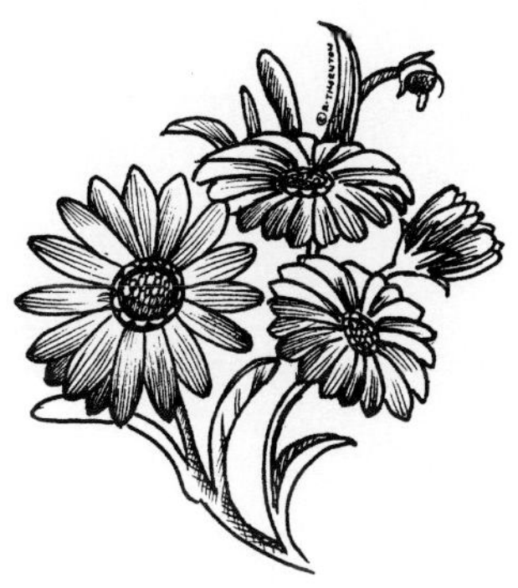

Country Sample Board

The sample board is a good beginner's project. In each square I have painted a different design to practise shading, stippling and liner work.

When finished, this little piece looks good in any country kitchen: on the wall or used as a pot stand.

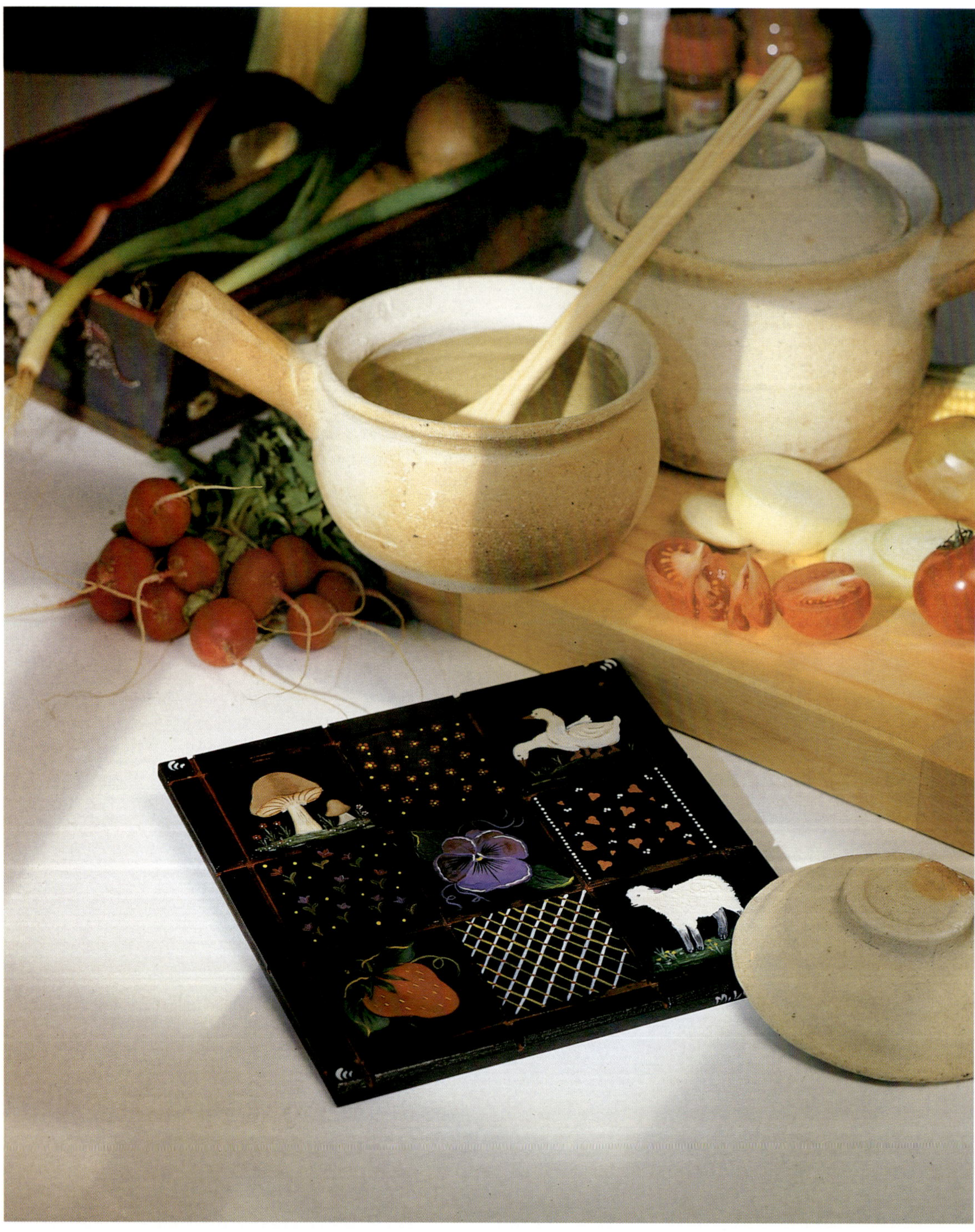

Palette
Yellows: Yellow Oxide, Yellow Light
Reds: Napthol Crimson, Burgundy
Greens: Pine Green, Green Oxide, Pthalo Green
Whites: Warm White, Smoked Pearl
Black: Carbon Black
Orange: Norwegian Orange
Purple: Diox. Purple
Browns: Fawn, Brown Earth

Medium
Jo Sonja satin polyurethane varnish (oil-based).

Brushes
No. 3 round brush
No. 1 liner brush
Old scrubby brush for stippling
No. 24 flat basecoat brush

PREPARATION

Sand the board lightly, especially inside the grooves.

Basecoat Carbon Black with a basecoat brush, sanding lightly between coats.

Paint inside the grooves with Napthol Crimson.

Transfer the pattern using white graphite paper.

PAINTING SQUARES

Mushroom

Stalk: Carbon Black

Cap: Fawn. Shade with Brown Earth using a round brush. Paint under the cap with Smoked Pearl and float some Brown Earth along the edges under the cap.

Liner work is done with Brown Earth using the liner brush.

Flower: Dot with Napthol Crimson using a stylus. White dot in the centre.

Grass: Drybrush with a little Green Oxide.

Geese

Paint with Warm White. Shade with a little Fawn.

Beaks: Norwegian Orange.

Feet: Norwegian Orange.

Wings: Paint with thick Warm White. Fill up the brush with a lot of white paint and roll it off by turning the brush when painting.

Eyes: Carbon Black.

Details: Carbon Black.

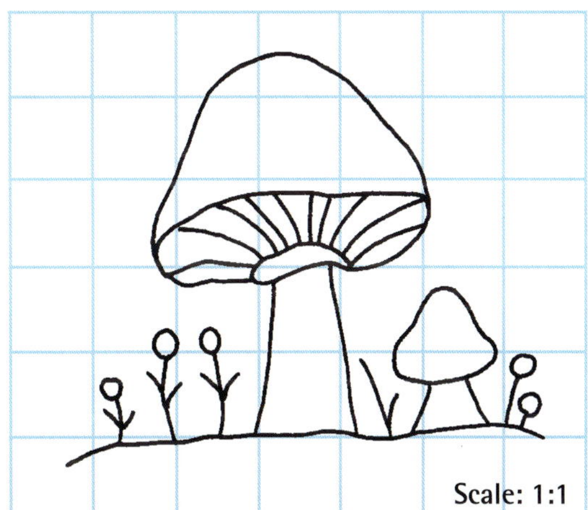

Scale: 1:1

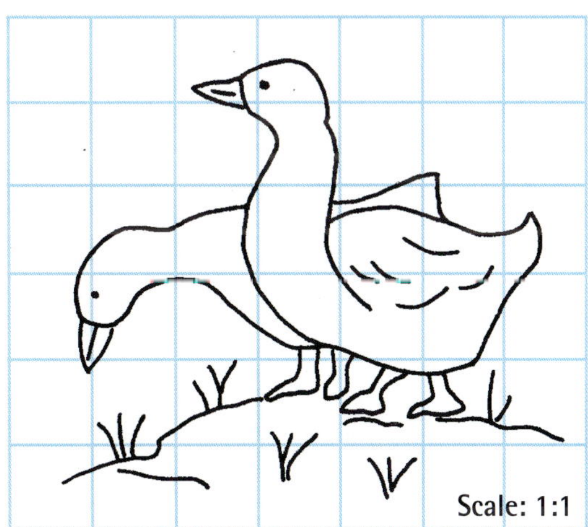

Scale: 1:1

Grass: Float some Pine Green under the geese and paint grass with the liner brush

Pansy

Basecoat: Diox. Purple mixed with Warm White.

Petal detail: Make washes of Burgundy and Diox. Purple on the palette and use the two colours in each petal. Let them run into each other slightly. Let dry.

Leaves: Paint with Green Oxide. Shade with Pine Green and pull turned edges with a load of Pine Green and Yellow Light, the lighter colour on the inside.

Finish the pansy by adding Carbon Black veins, a green dot for the centre, two white commas on the side and a yellow comma underneath the green dot.

Paint turned edges by loading a brush with Diox. Purple and Warm White (the white on the inside).

Lastly add line work with Diox. Purple.

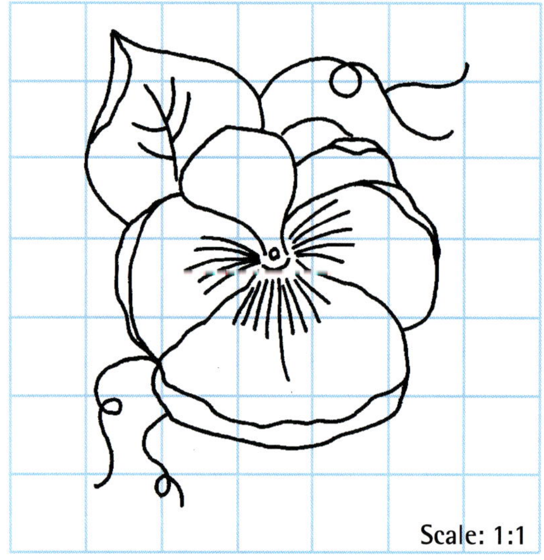

Scale: 1:1

Strawberry

Paint a first coat with Warm White, then two coats of Napthol Crimson.

Shade the strawberry by loading a brush with Burgundy. Paint halfway, then from the other side paint Napthol Crimson, blending the two in the middle.

Pat a little Norwegian Orange in the centre for a highlight.

Seeds: Little strokes of Carbon Black and Yellow Oxide.

Calyx: Paint with Green Oxide, shaded with a little Yellow Oxide.

Leaves: Shade with Pthalo Green. Turned edges are Pine Green and Yellow Oxide. Veins are Pine Green mixed with Carbon Black.

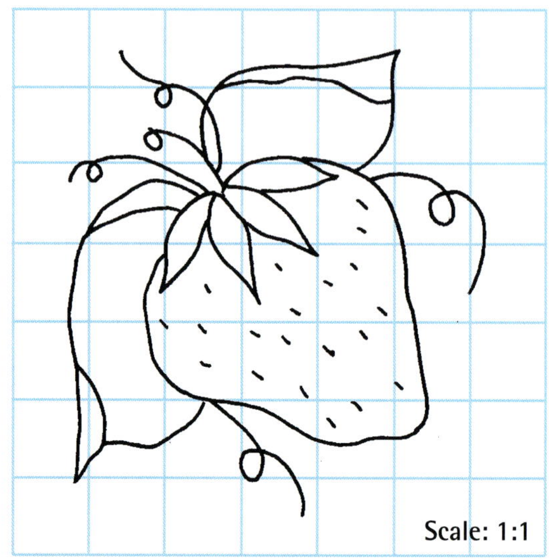

Scale: 1:1

Lamb

Body: Warm White.

Legs: Carbon Black mixed with Warm White.

Wool: Stipple with thick Warm White using an old brush.

Eye, mouth and nose: Carbon Black.

Grass: Pine Green.

Flowers: Yellow Light.

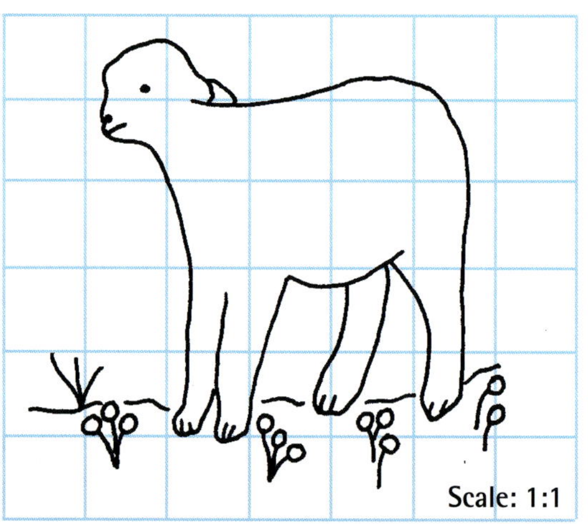

Scale: 1:1

Patchwork

Using a stylus, dot little flowers with Napthol Crimson and Yellow Light.

Tulips

Flowers are little commas with a double load of Diox. Purple and Napthol Crimson.

Leaves are commas with Green Oxide and Yellow Oxide.

'Dolly Parton' hearts

Using the end of a brush, place two dots next to each other. While the paint is still wet, pull the dots into a heart shape with the brush. Using a stylus, place small white dots in between the hearts.

Cross-hatching

Using the ruler, draw the cross-hatching on with a chalk pencil.

Paint fine lines with Warm White and Yellow Oxide on a liner brush. Where the lines cross, place a Napthol Crimson dot, using the stylus.

FINISHING

Erase all graphite lines with a soft eraser.

Varnish with two or three coats of oil-based polyurethane varnish for a durable finish.

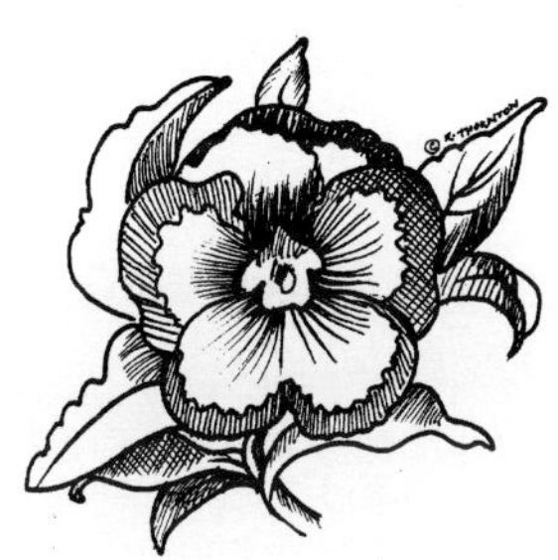

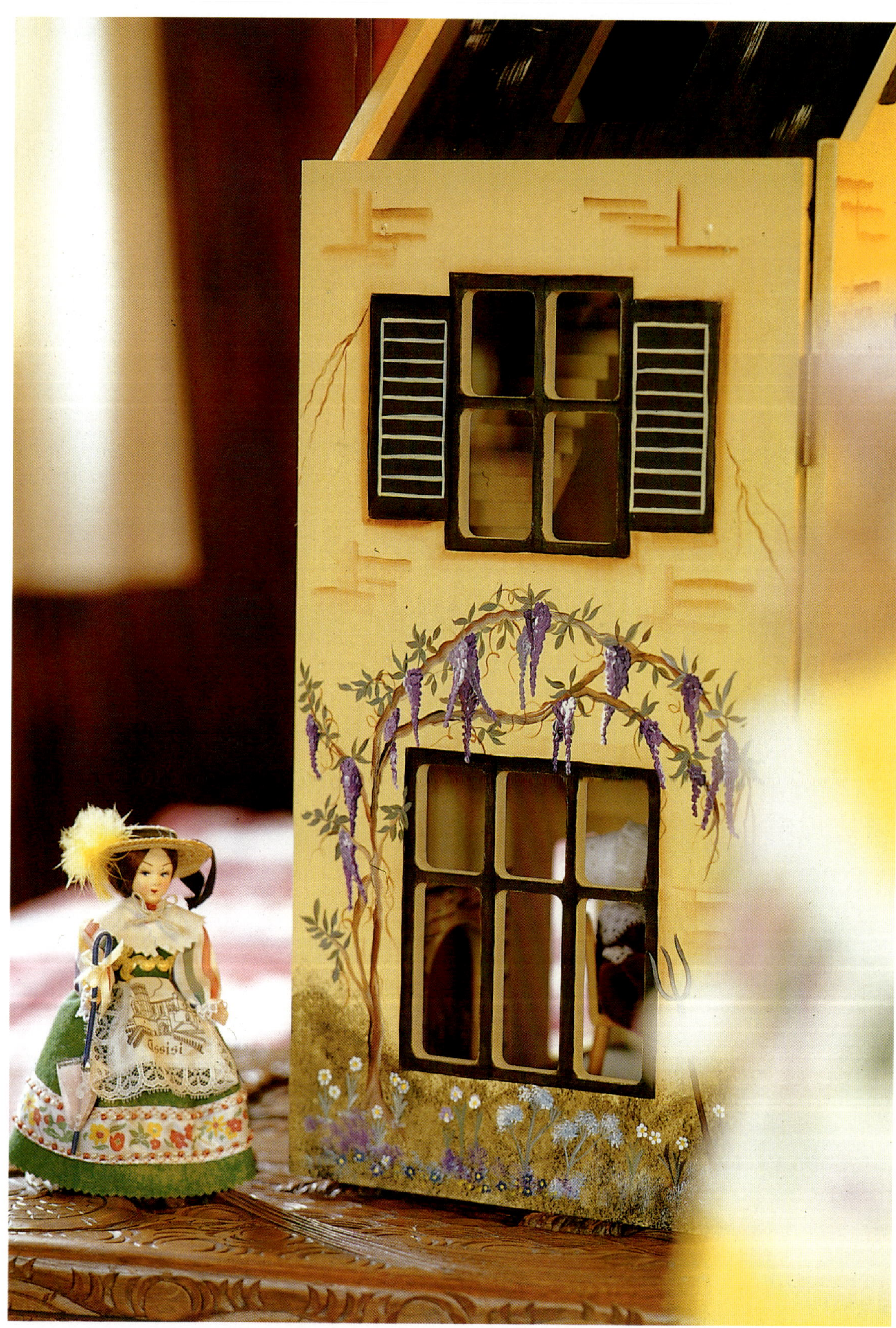

Dollshouse

The dollshouse used for this project is the Katie's Dollshouse produced by Ashford. There is a lot of scope for decorating both the inside and outside of this beautiful dollshouse – it is a lovely project to paint. I know children love bright colours and detail so I've painted a rose bush around the front door, flowers in the garden and a quilt airing on the washing line. Now all that's needed is the child to play with it!

Palette
Yellows: Yellow Light, Primrose (Plaid)
Brown: Brown Earth
Greens: Teal Green, Pthalo Green, Pine Green, Green Oxide, Southern Pine (Plaid)
Orange: Norwegian Orange
Reds: Burgundy, Napthol Crimson
Blue: Colony Blue
Whites: Warm White, Smoked Pearl
Black: Carbon Black
Purple: Diox. Purple

Mediums
Jo Sonja Tannin Blocking Sealer for Wood
Jo Sonja Flow Medium
Jo Sonja satin polyurethane varnish (water-based or oil-based)

Brushes
No. 3 round watercolour brush
No. 1 round liner brush
No. 8 flat brush
1/4-inch deerfoot brush (or an old fuzzy brush)
No. 25 varnish brush

PREPARATION

Seal the rough sides of the customwood or craft-wood, i.e. the edges of the house and inside windows, with Tannin Blocking Sealer before basecoating. Sand to give a smoother finish.

Basecoat the walls inside and out with Primrose.

Basecoat the roofs and floors with Southern Pine.

Use three layers of basecoat and sand between the coats.

PAINTING

Refer to the section on general painting for the special techniques used.

House Exterior

Measure a 5mm border around the door and windows and draw a pencil line.

Paint inside the lines and across the windows with Southern Pine (three coats). When dry, float a shadow of Carbon Black in the windows.

Float a shadow around all the windows and doors using Brown Earth and Carbon Black.

Shutters

Measure a rectangle out from each side of all top windows – 4cm wide by 9.5cm deep. Draw in with ruler and basecoat with three coats of Southern Pine.

Paint the line work inside the shutters with a mix of Primrose and Smoked Pearl. Float a shadow of Carbon Black inside them.

Frieze

Trace the frieze on the top of the front of the Dollshouse. (*see over*) Basecoat with Southern Pine.

Float a shadow of Carbon Black inside the frieze. Outline using Carbon Black on a liner brush. The dots are Primrose.

Grass

Using a sea sponge, sponge around the house with the darker greens first, finishing with light green, i.e Southern Pine, Pthalo Green, then Green Oxide. (I also sponged under the top windows to suggest window-boxes.)

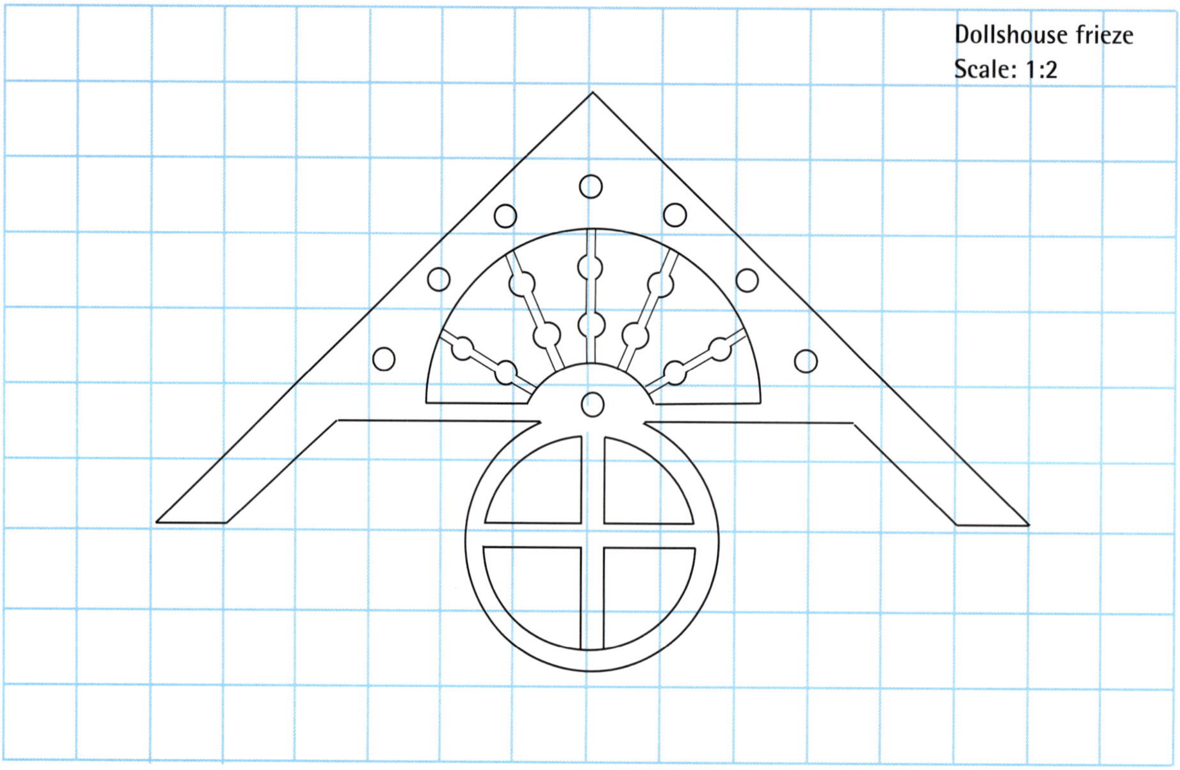

Dollshouse frieze
Scale: 1:2

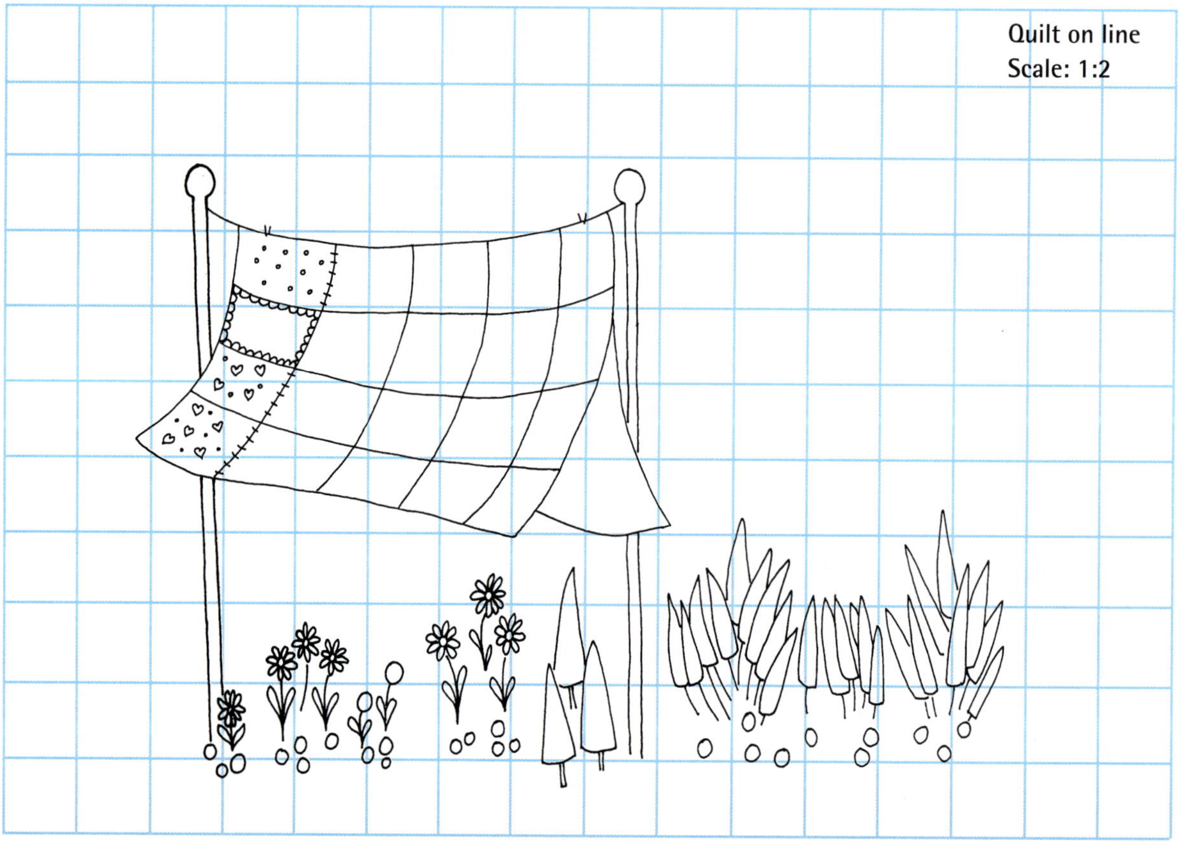

Quilt on line
Scale: 1:2

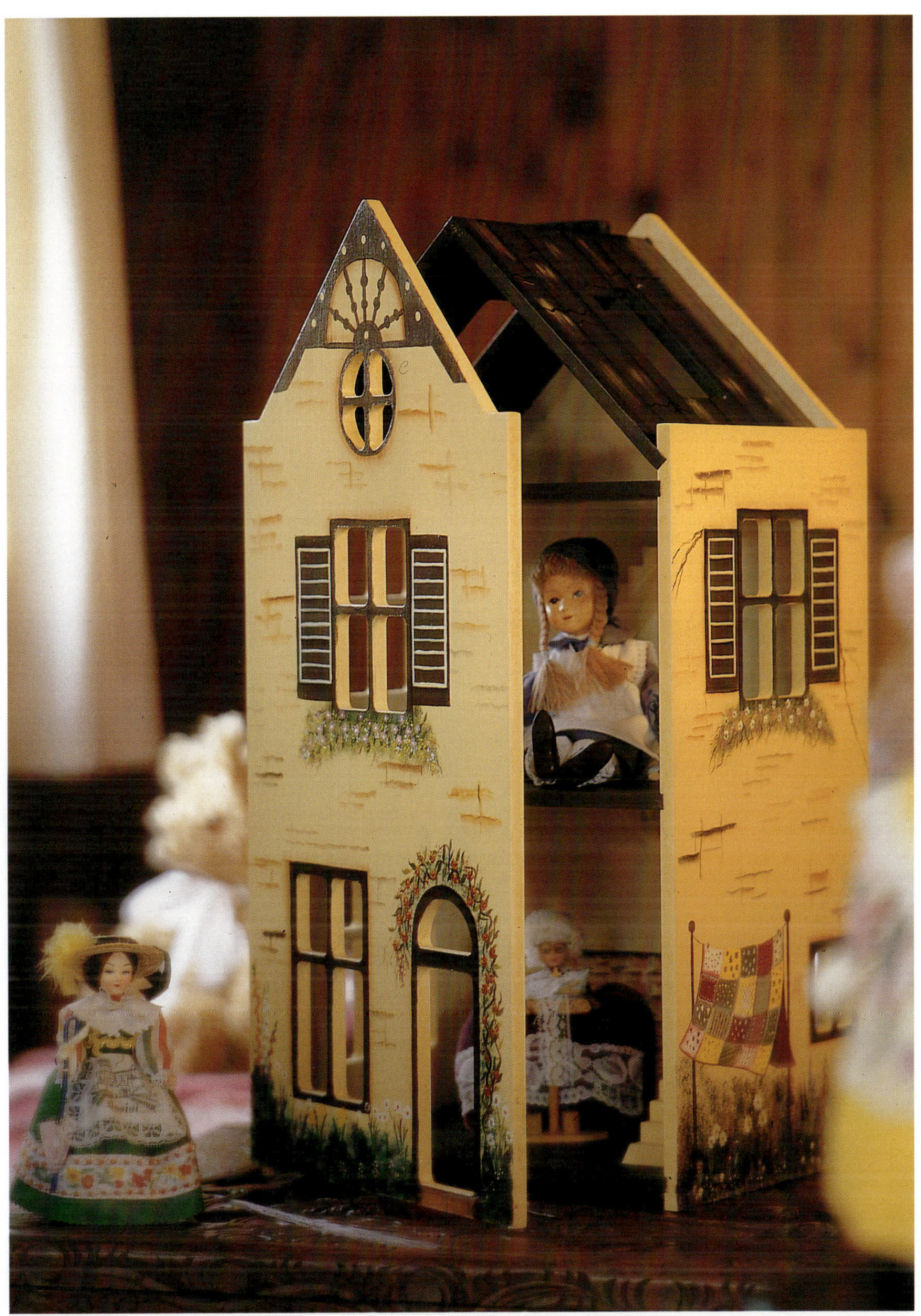

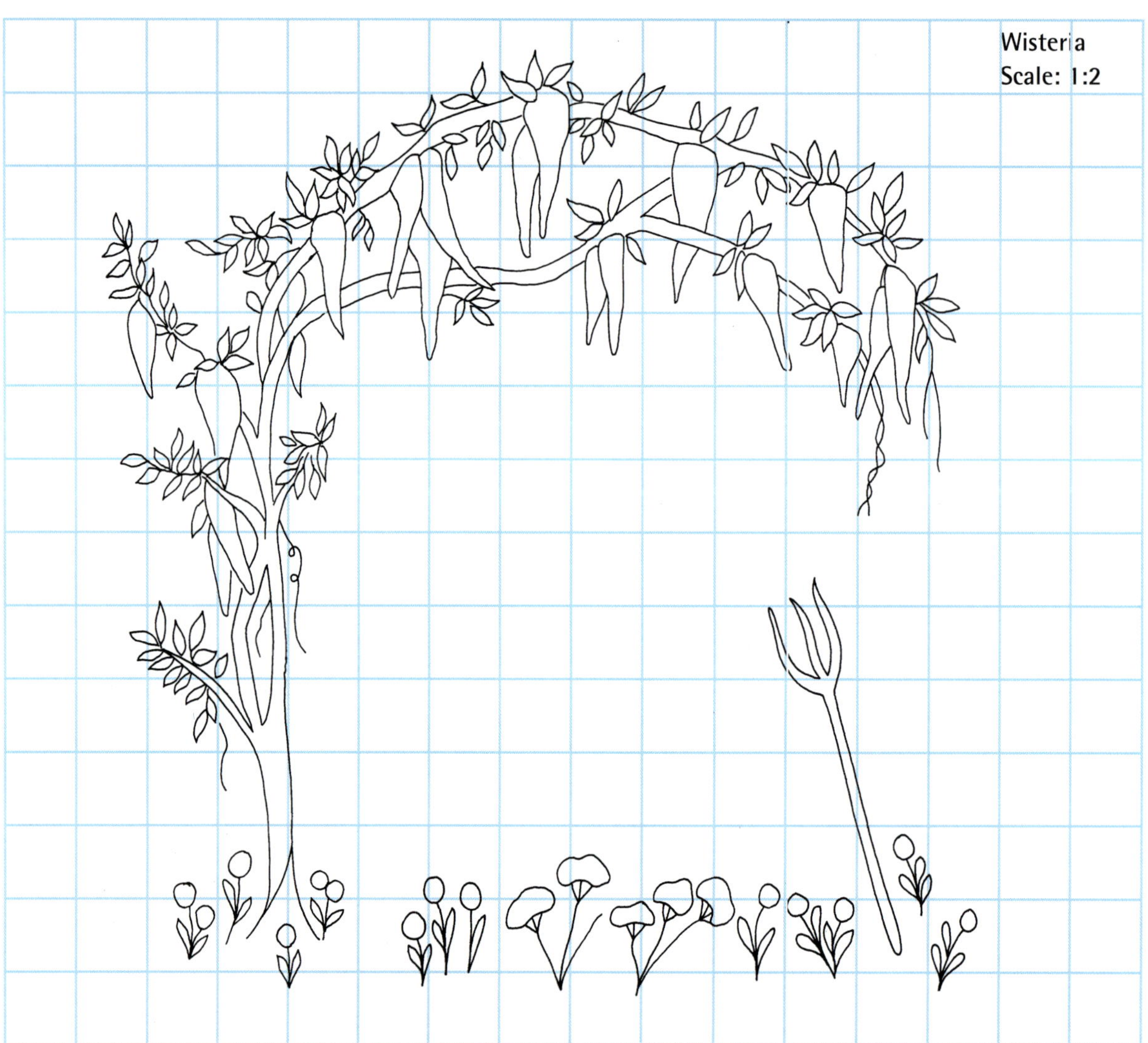

Wisteria

Branches and trunk: Double-load with Brown Earth and Warm White, sometimes a little Carbon Black.

Leaves: Green Oxide mixed with Warm White. Use Pine Green for darker leaves.

Flowers: Dot with Diox. Purple and Warm White. Shade with a mix of Diox. Purple and Carbon Black.

Rose bush

Sponge around the front door with light green (Green Oxide mixed with Warm White).

Branches: Brown Earth mixed with Pine Green.

Leaves: Pine Green and Green Oxide.

Veins: Pull these with Brown Earth.

Roses: Basecoat with Burgundy. Overstroke with small commas in Yellow Light and Norwegian Orange.

Lastly, use a deerfoot brush to stipple a little Yellow Light between the roses.

Garden flowers

Daisies: Warm White with yellow centres/medium green leaves.

Foxgloves: Warm White with green centres/dark green leaves.

Daffodils: Yellow cup with Norwegian Orange centres.

Pink daisies (under the top windows): A mix of Burgundy and Warm White, with little white dots in between.

Bricks

A side-load of Brown Earth, sometimes mixed with Carbon Black.

Quilt

Basecoat squares with Yellow Light, Burgundy/Warm White and Green Oxide.

Paint some squares lighter by mixing Warm White with Green or Burgundy.

Float some colours inside the lighter or darker squares. Add details with a liner brush.

Paint the inside of the quilt with Burgundy, shade with Carbon Black and highlight with Warm White.

Washing line

Paint the poles a mixture of Brown Earth outlined with Carbon Black and Burgundy.

Lavender flowers

Green Oxide mixed with Warm White and different values of purple dotted with White and Colony Blue to create the flowers.

Fork

Brown Earth and grey (mix Carbon Black and Warm White).

Chimney bricks

Using a large flat brush, double-load with Norwegian Orange and Brown Earth. Line work with a mix of Carbon Black and Brown Earth.

Float a shadow of Carbon Black around the outside. Use Carbon Black for the line work on the top.

Roof

Float with Carbon Black to create dark shadows from top to bottom.

Line work with Brown Earth and Carbon Black. Add a little highlight with Warm White.

House Interior

Fireplace surround

Double load of Burgundy and Brown Earth.

Line work with Carbon Black and Brown Earth.

Flames

Napthol Crimson and Yellow Light.

FINISHING

Two to three coats of water-based polyurethane varnish.

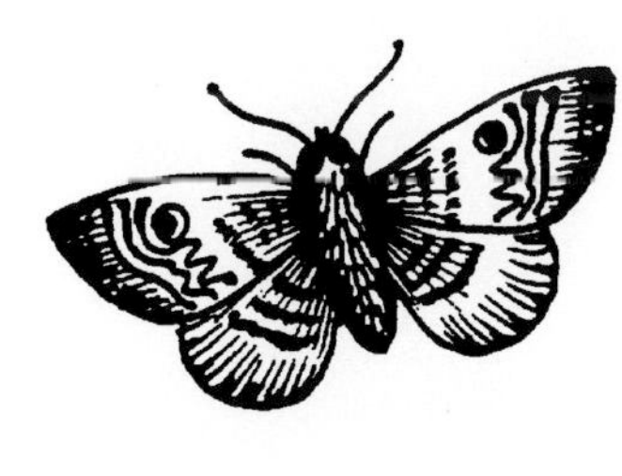

Cutlery Tray

The true purpose for this decorative and useful kitchen item may be to hold your knives, forks and spoons, but that's not its only role in my kitchen! It is also used by my children as a safe place to store treasure: little shells collected on the beach, tiny beads fallen from a much-loved necklace.

The design was inspired by the quilt on our bed and I have used fruits, vegetables and lettering to give the tray an olde worlde look.

Palette
Yellows: Yellow Light, Yellow Oxide
Brown: Brown Earth
Greens: Pine Green, Green Oxide
Reds: Burgundy, Napthol Red Light
White: Warm White
Blue: French Blue
Gold: Rich Gold
Black: Carbon Black

Mediums
Jo Sonja Flow Medium
Jo Sonja satin polyurethane varnish (oil-based)
Burnt Umber oil paint
Artist's turpentine

Brushes
No. 25 flat basecoating brush
No. 3 round brush
No. 8 flat brush
No. 0 line brush

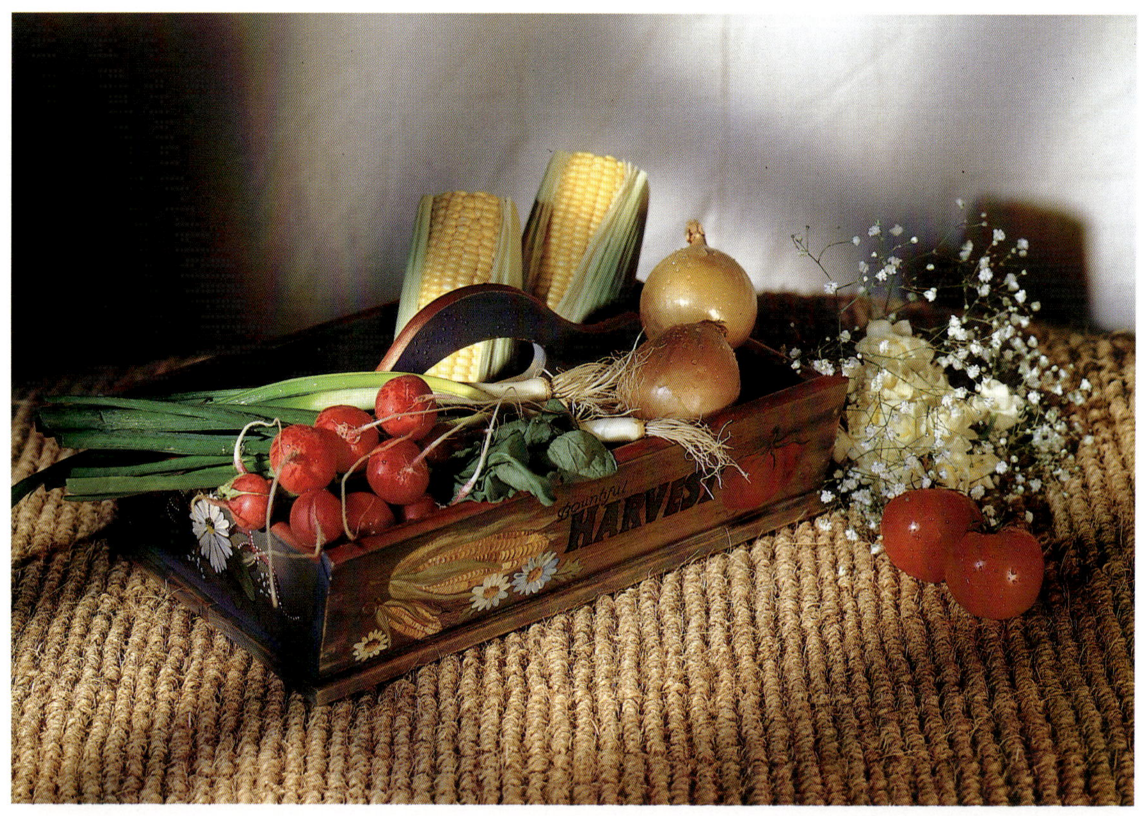

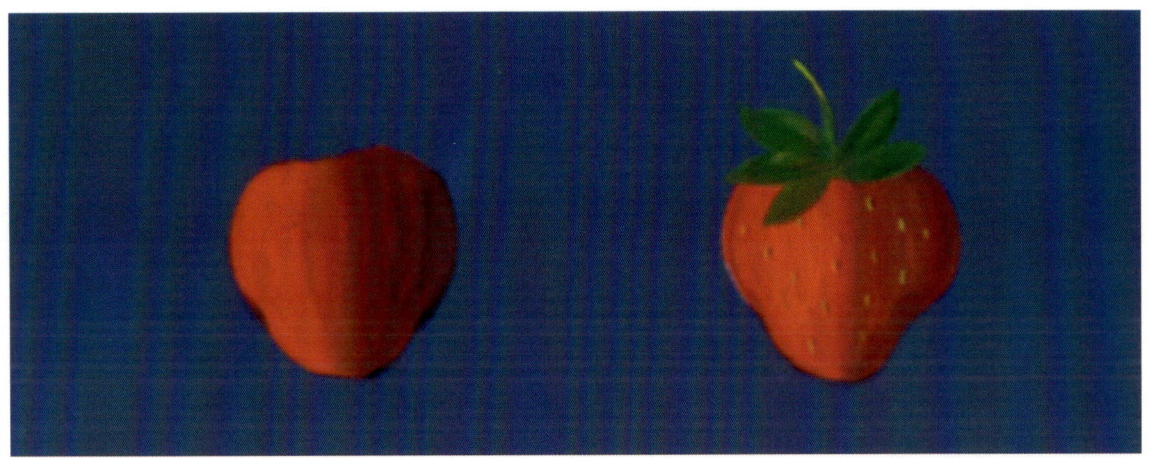

PREPARATION

Fill the nail holes with a pine wood filler.

Lightly sand the cutlery tray. Wipe off the dust with a tackcloth.

Mix French Blue with water 5:1 (it is better to start with a lighter mixture).

Use an old piece of lint-free material and dip into the water/paint mixture. Start to rub it on the tray in the direction of the grain – the grain should show through.

Do the whole tray inside and out. Let it dry thoroughly. If the finish is not satisfactory, rub on a second coat.

Sand the tray to a smooth finish with fine sandpaper. Seal with Jo Sonja Glazing Medium.

Transfer the pattern on with white graphite paper.

PAINTING

Side 1

Strawberries

Basecoat with Warm White. Let dry.

Second-coat with Napthol Red Light.

On the left side of the strawberry, stroke halfway across in Burgundy. On the right side, stroke halfway across with Napthol Red Light. Blend the two colours together in the centre.

If you find this is difficult, use a little Flow Medium on your brush to make the blending easier. When you blend, use long strokes. Don't pat the surface or you will lift off the paint.

Stroke in highlights of Yellow Light or Green Oxide on the right side of the strawberry.

Seeds: Small strokes with Yellow Oxide and Burgundy. Use a liner brush.

Leaves: Basecoat with Green Oxide.

Shade with Pine Green on the bottom half and highlight with a mix of Green Oxide and Yellow Oxide on the top half.

Use a mix of Yellow Light and Green Oxide to paint the veins.

Calyx: Basecoat with Green Oxide. Shade with Pine Green.

Highlight with a mix of Yellow Light and Green Oxide.

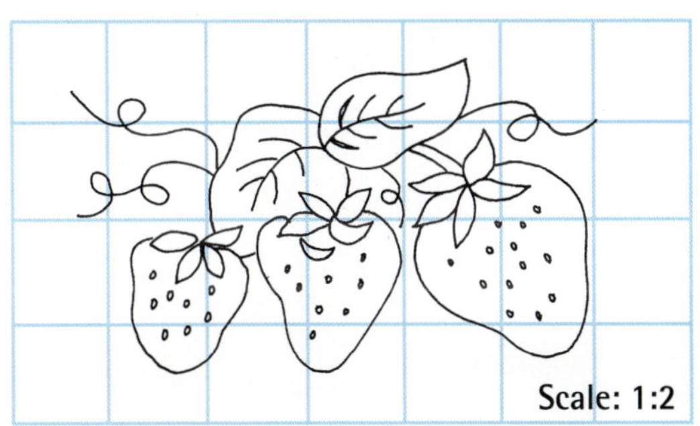

Scale: 1:2

Lettering

Paint with Burgundy.

Outline with Carbon Black using a liner brush.

Remembering when pulling fine line work to water down the paint until it is the consistency of ink, so the paint flows off your brush more easily. Also, hold the brush upright (perpendicular to the surface).

Stroke in a little Rich Gold in the capital letters.

Basket

Basecoat with Brown Earth.

Pull little strokes of Yellow Oxide and Carbon Black.

Paint the rim with Yellow Oxide and Brown Earth using little S strokes.

Outline with Carbon Black.

Fruit and vegetables

Corn: Yellow Oxide, Brown Earth, Green Oxide.

Spring onions: Warm White, Green Oxide.

Apples: Napthol Red Light, Green Oxide.

Pears: Yellow Oxide and a little Green Oxide.

Onions: Napthol Red Light mixed with a little Brown Earth.

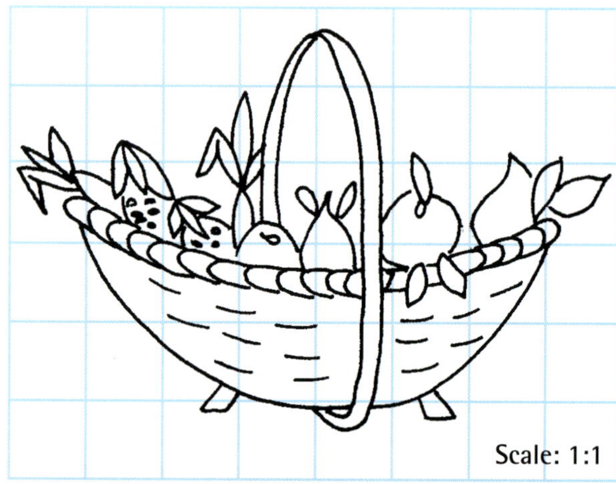

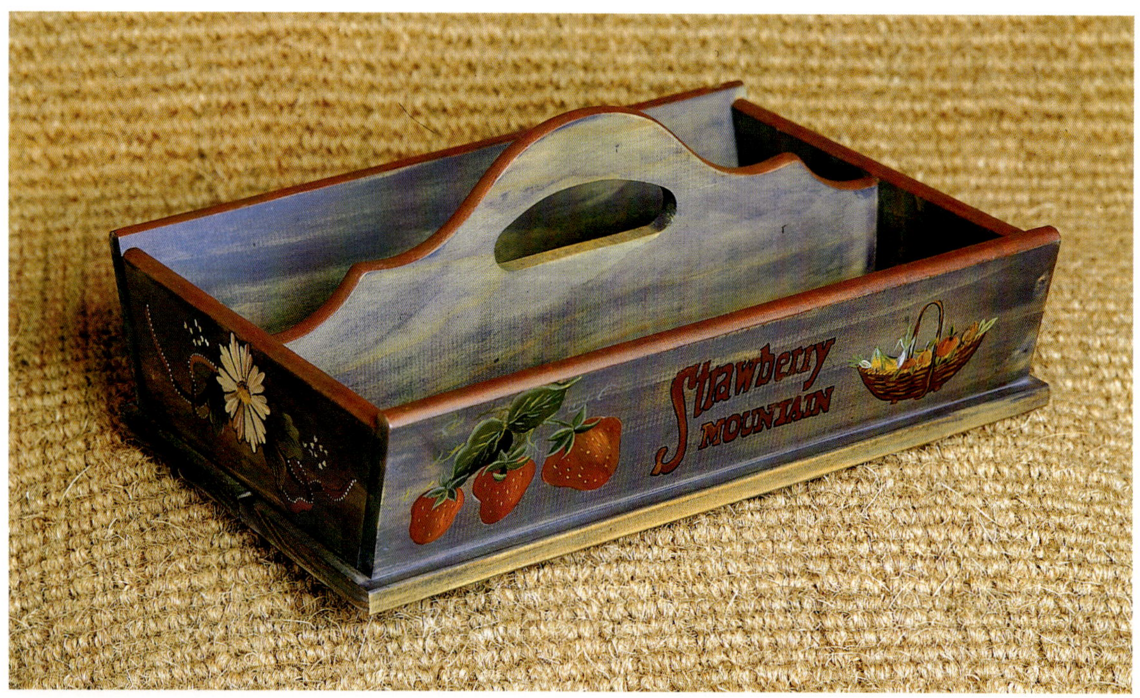

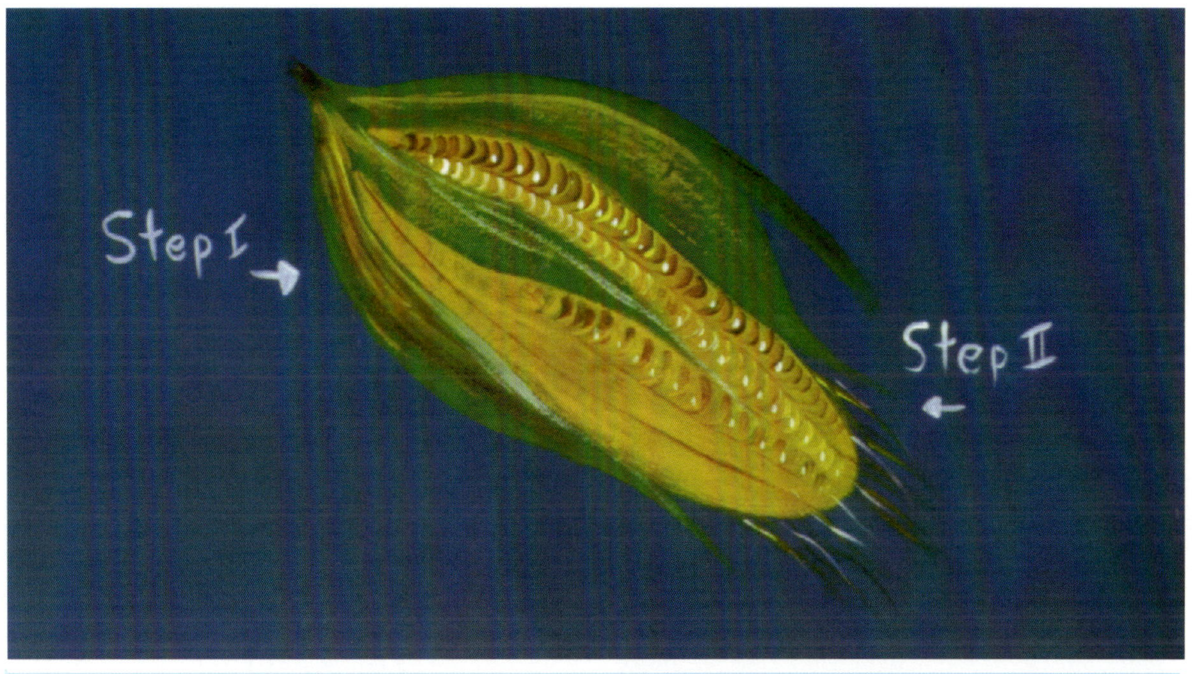

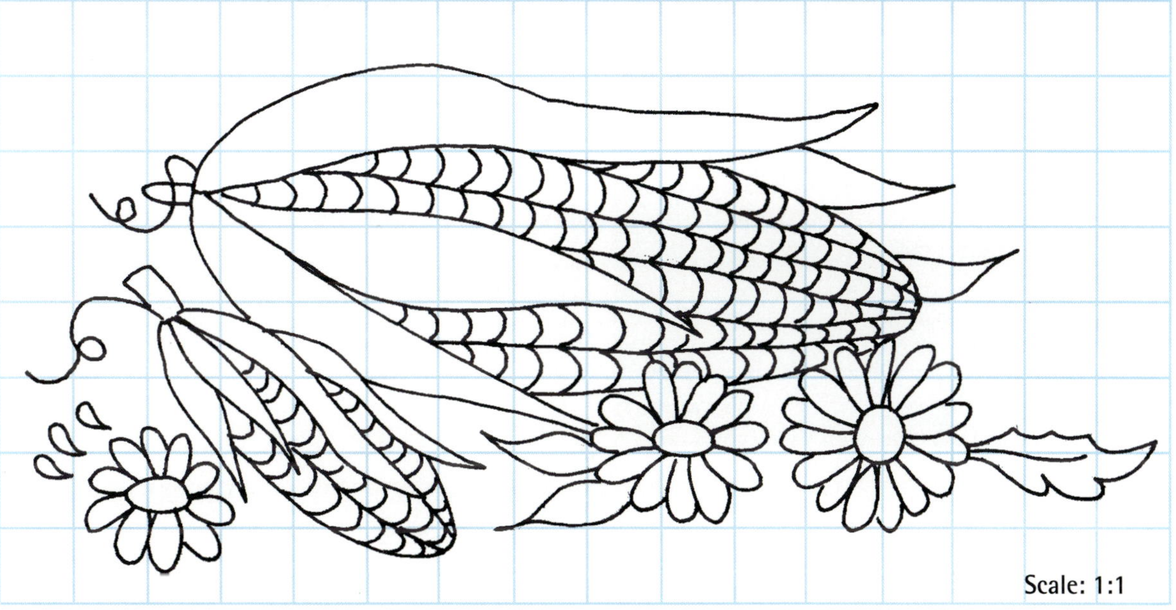

Scale: 1:1

Side 2

Corn

Basecoat with Yellow Oxide.

Using a No. 3 brush, paint little C strokes to create kernels.

Double-load your brush with Yellow Light and Brown Earth, or Yellow Light and Warm White, and paint little strokes on the corn graduating from small at the top to larger at the bottom.

Highlight the kernels with little dots of Warm White.

Husk: Basecoat with Green Oxide.

Dry-brush on top with Yellow Light and Brown Earth to create shading.

Use Green Oxide to create stems at the top of the husk.

Outline with Brown Earth.

Bountiful HARVEST

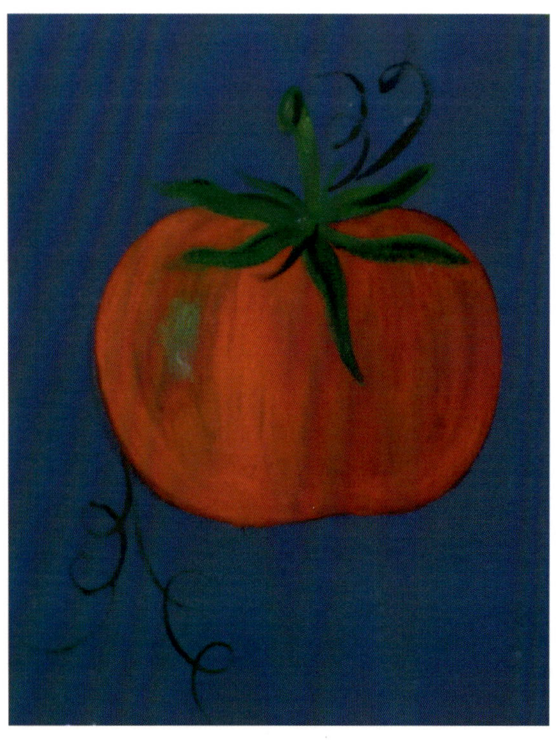

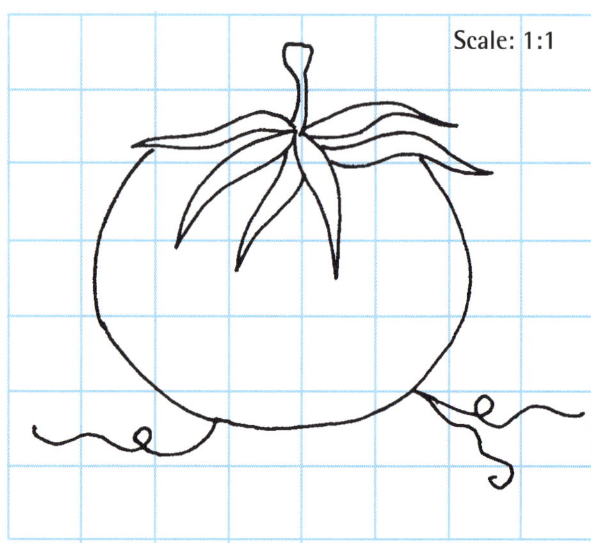

Lettering

Small: Carbon Black.

Large: French Blue.

Outline with Carbon Black.

Float Carbon Black on the inside of the letters on the left side.

Tomato

Basecoat with Napthol Red Light.

Shade with a mix of Napthol Red Light and Burgundy.

Drybrush some Green Oxide on the sides to create a rounded effect.

Highlight with a little Warm White. Use strokes of different values of green for the top and stem using Green Oxide, Yellow Oxide and Pine Green.

Line work with Brown Earth.

Sides 3 and 4

Ribbons

Basecoat with Burgundy.

Highlight with a mix of Burgundy and Warm White.

Shade with a mix of Burgundy and Carbon Black.

Use the same blending technique as for the strawberries. By adding Carbon Black or Warm White

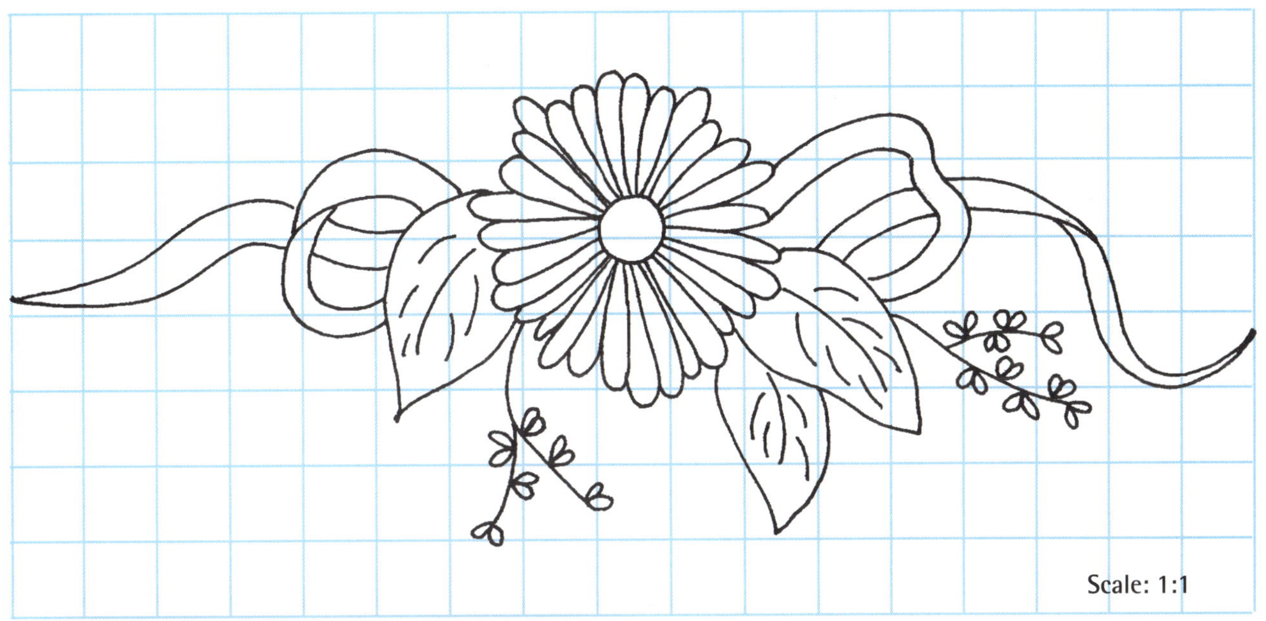

Scale: 1:1

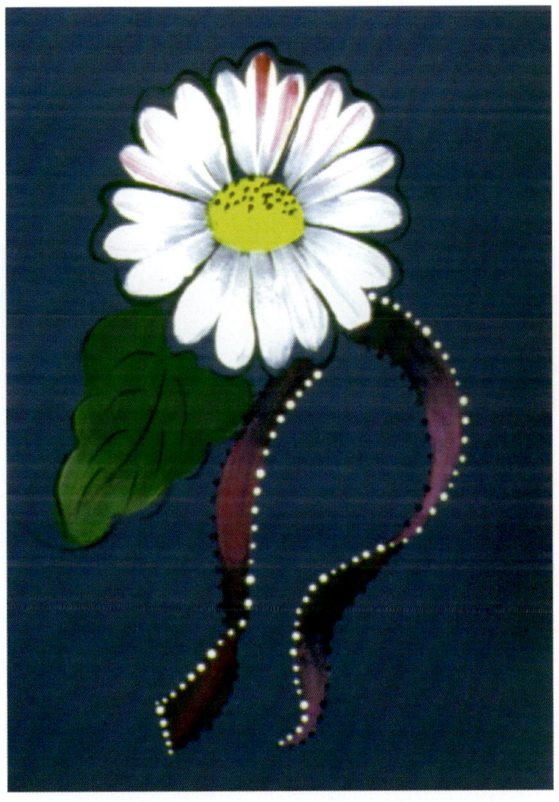

Leaves

Basecoat with Green Oxide.

Shade with Pine Green.

Highlight with Pine Green mixed with Warm White (use the blending technique).

Veins are Carbon Black.

Daisies

Petals: Three teardrop strokes in Warm White, with a little Burgundy sometimes picked up at the end of the brush.

Outline with Carbon Black. (Stop and start with the outlining – it should look very casual.)

Centre: Yellow Light.
Carbon Black dots on top half of centre.

Small Flowers

Stems: Green Oxide.

Flowers: Little strokes of Warm White.

Edges of Tray

Use an old round brush to paint with a mix of Burgundy and Rich Gold.

you can create a darker or lighter value of colour.

Create dots with Warm White and Carbon Black (cross over where the ribbon turns). To make nice round dots, use a small stylus or kebab stick.

33

FINISHING

Mix Burnt Umber Oil Paint with artist's turpentine until you have a creamy consistency (1:4).

Use an old lint-free cloth and rub this antiquing medium on lightly to soften and mellow the colours. (Test first on the bottom of the tray for the right consistency.)

If the antiquing is too dark, remove it with atist's turpentine.

Let it dry for a couple of days.

Finish with two to three coats of polyurethane varnish (oil-based).

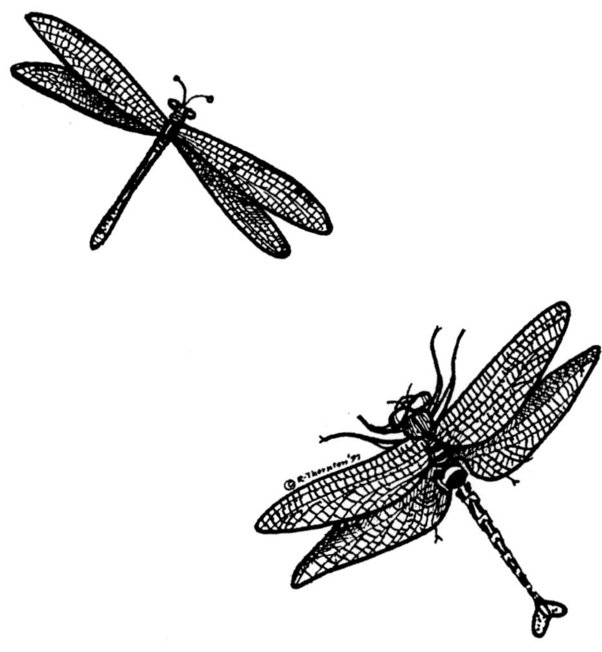

Sailing Ship on a Large Pine Tray

Ko te mea nui? He tangata, he tangata, he tangata.
(What is the most important thing? It is people, it is people, it is people.)

When I sit upstairs in my workroom, at home in Diamond Harbour, I often watch the yachts racing. I love the view over the harbour and out to the ocean; sometimes I picture one of the first four ships sailing into the harbour with settlers from Britain in 1840s, and I wonder what their thoughts and dreams would have been when they saw the hills of the harbour.

I have done a painting based on those first sailing ships and have used Maori designs as decorative border patterns.

The diamond design is patiki, the flounder, which is woven into the tukutuku panels that line the walls of meeting houses. My son Paul often catches flounder when he goes fishing off the local wharf.

I also painted the koru, a shape that is linked to the fern plant, which has a curled-over tip and unfurls to become the full-sized fern plant. It is a symbol of growth, life and movement.

Palette
Whites: Warm White, Smoked Pearl, Soft White
    (background colour)
Black: Carbon Black
Browns: Burnt Umber, Brown Earth
Greens: Pine Green, Teal Green
Blues: Aqua, Sapphire
Yellow: Yellow Oxide
Purple: Amethyst
Red: Spice (background colour)

Mediums
Jo Sonja Decor Crackle Medium
Burnt Umber oil paint
Artist's turpentine
Jo Sonja satin polyurethane varnish (oil-based)

Brushes
No. 25 basecoat flat brush
No. 8 flat brush
No. 3 round brush
No. 1 liner brush
Soft varnishing brush

PREPARATION

I have used a large pine tray from Ashford Handicrafts.

Basecoat the inside of the tray with Soft White as a background colour. Let dry and sand with fine sandpaper.

Apply an even coat of Jo Sonja Decor Crackle Medium to the inside of the tray with a soft flat brush. Allow to dry thoroughly.

Apply a coat of Spice as a background colour over the Crackle Medium – do not overbrush.

Basecoat the rest of the tray with two coats of Spice.

Seal with Clear Glazing Medium.

Sand back the edges of the tray to expose the wood grain.

Draw a chalk pencil line around the inside edge of the tray: 6cm in from the ends of the tray and 4cm in from the sides.

Draw another line, again using your chalk pencil, 6cm in from the bottom line you have drawn. This will be your horizon.

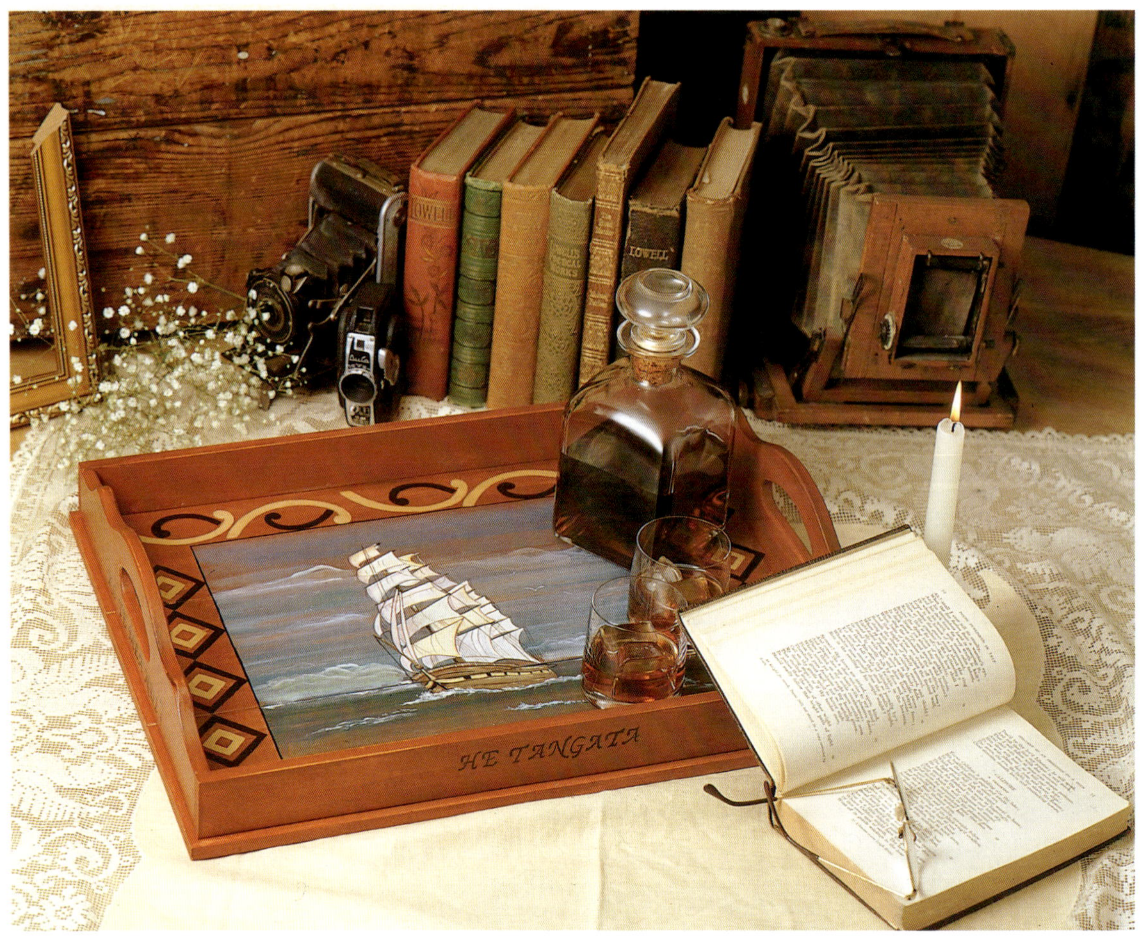

PAINTING

Background

Sky

Make a wash of watery paint on your palette using Aqua and Sapphire.

Mask off your chalk lines with magic tape.

Apply the wash of Aqua and Sapphire with long strokes, using a large flat brush. Let the colours blend slightly. Use gentle pressure on the brush to ensure that you don't lift the crackle.

Sea

Make a wash of Teal Green and mix it with a little Aqua. Apply as above.

Let dry completely.

Trace on the pattern using white graphite paper.

Ship

Hull

Two coats of Brown Earth.

Transfer the details.

Drybrush a Yellow Oxide stripe across the hull.

Mast

Brown Earth.

Sails

Warm White. With a flat brush, use the floating technique to shade the sails with Amethyst, Yellow Oxide and Sapphire mixed with Amethyst.

Outline with Brown Earth mixed with a little Carbon Black.

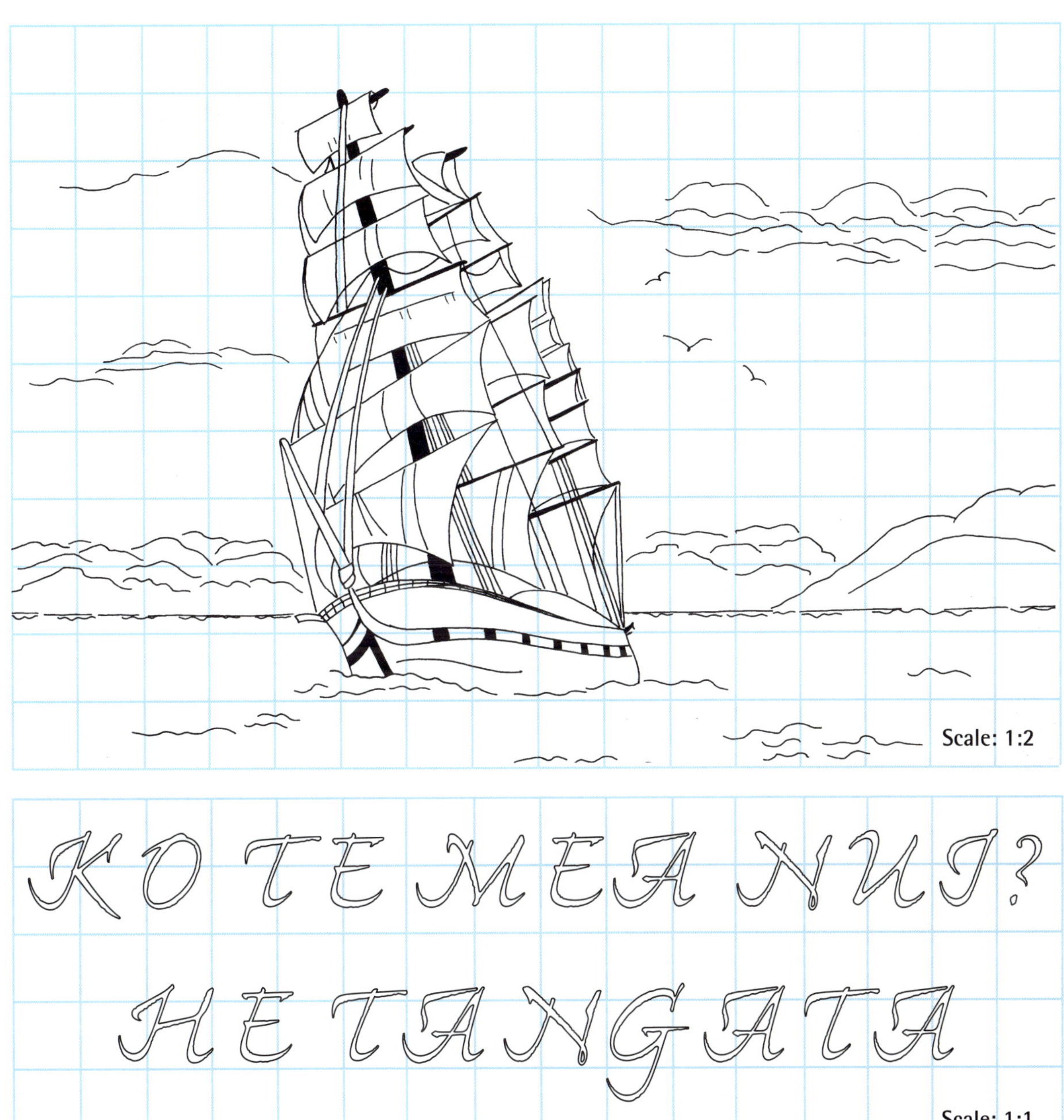

Rigging
Brown Earth using a liner brush.

Portholes and beams
Carbon Black.

Waves
Aqua and Warm White. Drybrush.

Hills
Pine Green and shaded with Yellow Oxide.

Clouds
Washes of Aqua and Warm White, some mixed with a little Yellow Oxide. Keep them transparent.

Seagulls
Warm White.

Maori Patterns

Patiki (four times)

Outside pattern with Carbon Black.

Inside pattern with Smoked Pearl.

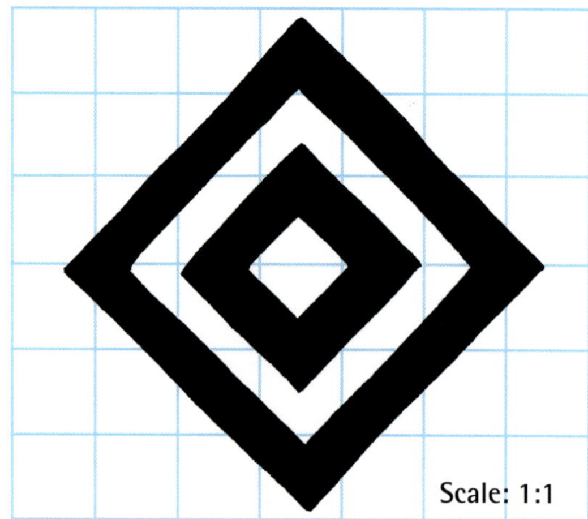

Scale: 1:1

Koru (five times)

Short koru with Carbon Black.

Long koru with Smoked Pearl.

Lettering

Trace the lettering around the outside of the tray
using white graphite paper.

Paint with Carbon Black using a liner brush.

Outline the painting with Carbon Black.

ANTIQUING

I antiqued the Maori border patterns lightly using
Burnt Umber oil paint and artist's turpentine. Let it
dry for a couple of days.

VARNISHING

Two coats of oil-based polyurethane varnish.

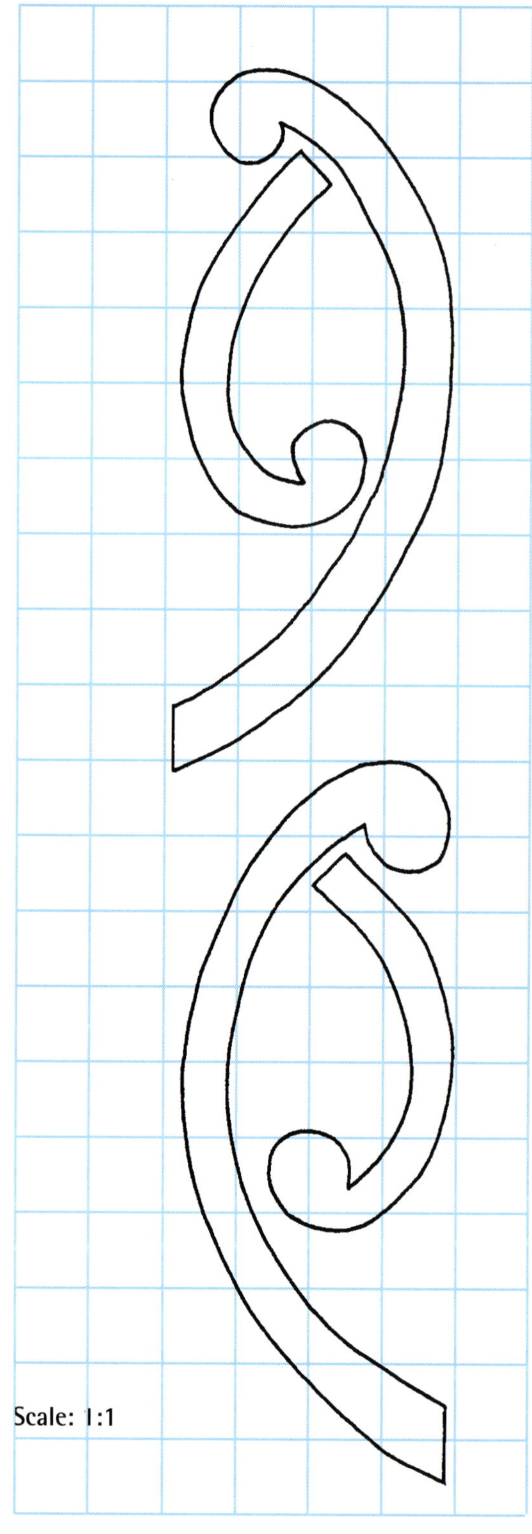

Scale: 1:1

Traditional Spinning Wheel and Spinning Chair

This beautiful spinning chair and wheel are manufactured in rimu, a New Zealand timber, by Ashfords. We chose these two items for the book because they are synonymous not only with the Ashford name but also with New Zealand: all those sheep – millions of them – and our fine wool and wool products.

In the past, spinning wheels in Europe were often decorated in various folk art styles. The decorations were simple and stylised as this was not only a decorative piece but a functional household object.

I decided to stain the wheel and chair and decorate them with scroll work and stylised flowers inspired by the Norwegian Rosemaling.

Palette
Yellow: Yellow Oxide
Red: Burgundy
Green: Teal Green
White: Smoked Pearl
Black: Carbon Black

Mediums
Jo Sonja satin polyurethane varnish
   (oil-based)

Brushes
No. 3 round brush
No. 1 round liner brush
No. 8 flat brush
No. 25 varnish brush

PREPARATION

Mix Teal Green 1:5 with water on an old saucer to make a watery stain.

Using an old lint-free cloth, rub a light coat of the stain onto every part of the spinning wheel and chair. (You can also use a soft No. 25 flat brush to do this.) Let dry.

Sand with fine sandpaper.

If necessary apply a second coat.

Sand the pieces until the wood feels very smooth – this will make it easier to paint.

PAINTING

Spinning Wheel

Use white graphite paper to transfer the patterns onto the spinning wheel parts.

Treadle assembly

Basecoat the large scrolls and leaves with two coats of Teal Green.

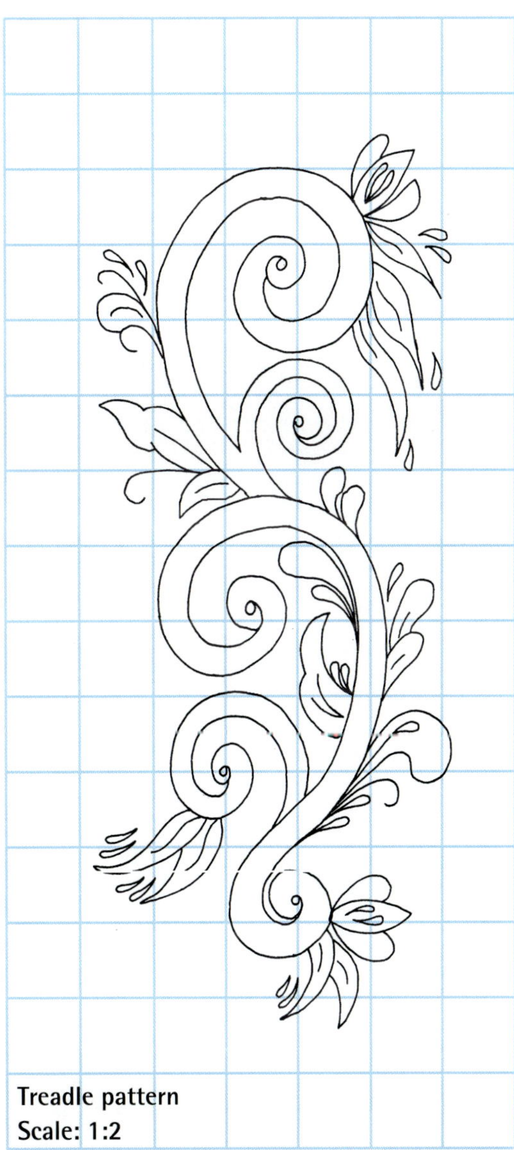

Treadle pattern
Scale: 1:2

Side-load a flat brush with Smoked Pearl and blend it on your palette. Highlight the inside of the scroll with floated colour.

Side-load the brush with Carbon Black and shade the outside of the scrolls with floated colour.

Use a liner brush to outline the highlighted side with Smoked Pearl and the shaded side with Carbon Black.

With a liner brush continue into the head of the scroll on the shaded side and paint a black dot.

Highlight and shade the green leaves with Smoked Pearl and Carbon Black.

Outline with Carbon Black.

Paint the veins with Carbon Black.

Double-load a round brush with Burgundy and Yellow Oxide to paint the stylised flowers and the big commas.

Outline the flowers with Carbon Black and paint some smaller commas in the centre.

Paint the red leaves with Burgundy, highlighted with Yellow Oxide on the top side.

Outline with Carbon Black.

Paint the smaller scrolls on the opposite side, and the commas, with Carbon Black.

Maiden bar

Basecoat in Yellow Oxide.

The scrolls on each side are basecoated with Teal Green.

Side-load a No. 8 flat brush with Smoked Pearl. Blend on your palette. Highlight the inside of the scrolls, around the centre of each petal and the edges of the flower with this floated colour.

Side-load with Carbon Black and shade the outside of the scrolls.

Using Carbon Black on a liner brush, outline the shaded side of the scrolls and the flower.

Using Smoked Pearl on a liner brush, paint commas on the inside of the scroll and place dots around the centre of the flower.

All other commas are painted with Carbon Black.

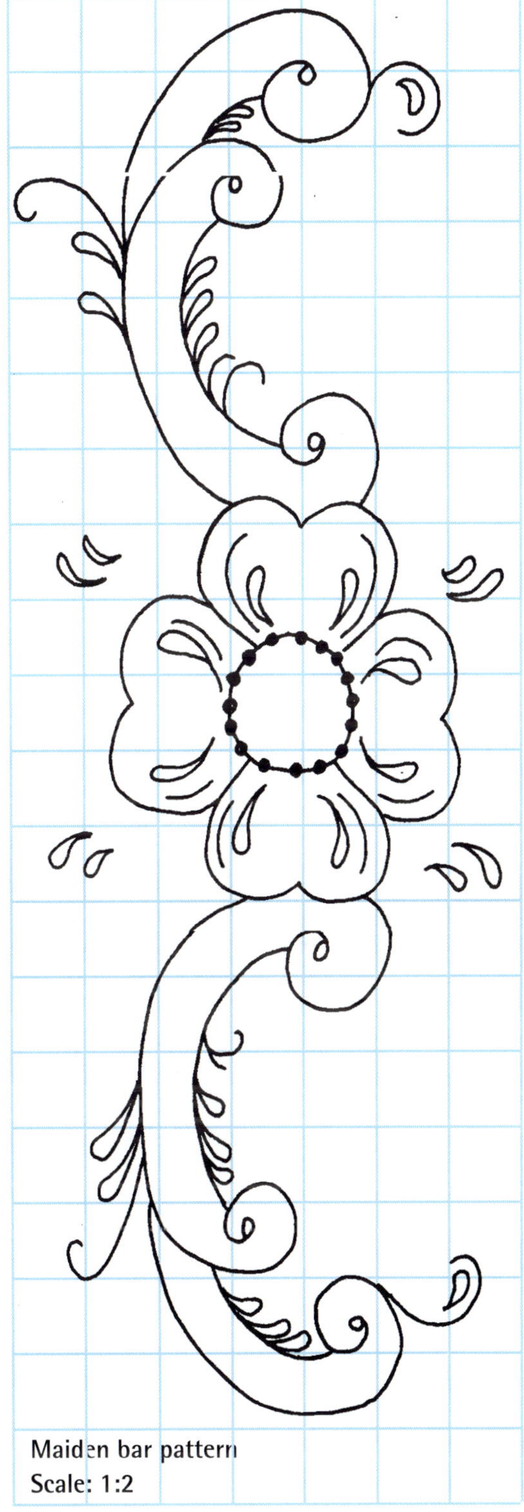

Maiden bar pattern
Scale: 1:2

Single leg (Spinning Wheel)

Basecoat the scroll with Teal Green.

Work as above for shading and highlighting.

The commas, flowers and leaves are a double load
of Burgundy and Yellow Oxide.

All the liner work and small commas are done with
Carbon Black.

Side-rails and wheel support legs

These are both painted with the scroll design at right.
Continue the pattern down the support legs and
along the side-rails.

Use a liner brush and water down the Teal Green
slightly so it flows off the bristles.

Hold the brush upright to paint the scroll.

Paint the commas on both sides of the scrolls with
a double load of Yellow Oxide and Burgundy.

The dots are Burgundy.

Lazy Kate

Flower: Basecoat with Yellow Oxide.

Scrolls: Teal Green.

Leaves: A mixture of Teal Green and Yellow Oxide.

Centre leaf: Burgundy.

Line work: Carbon Black and Smoked Pearl.

Commas: Carbon Black and Smoked Pearl.

Highlighting and shading: As above.

Spinning Chair

Seat back

Basecoat the large scrolls with Teal Green (follow
instructions for treadle assembly).

Highlight on the inside with Smoked Pearl.

Shade on the outside with Carbon Black.

Outline with Smoked Pearl on the highlighted side.

Outline with Carbon Black on the shaded side.

Small scrolls: Basecoat with Yellow Oxide.

Shade with Burgundy.

Outline with Carbon Black.

Paint the dots with Burgundy.

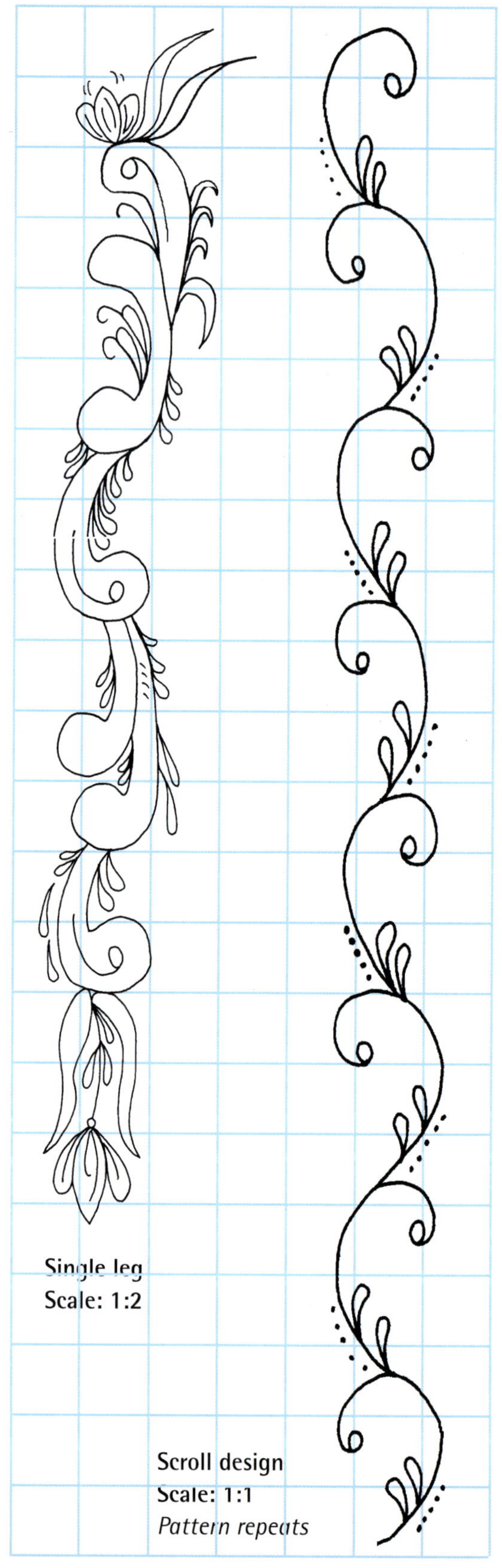

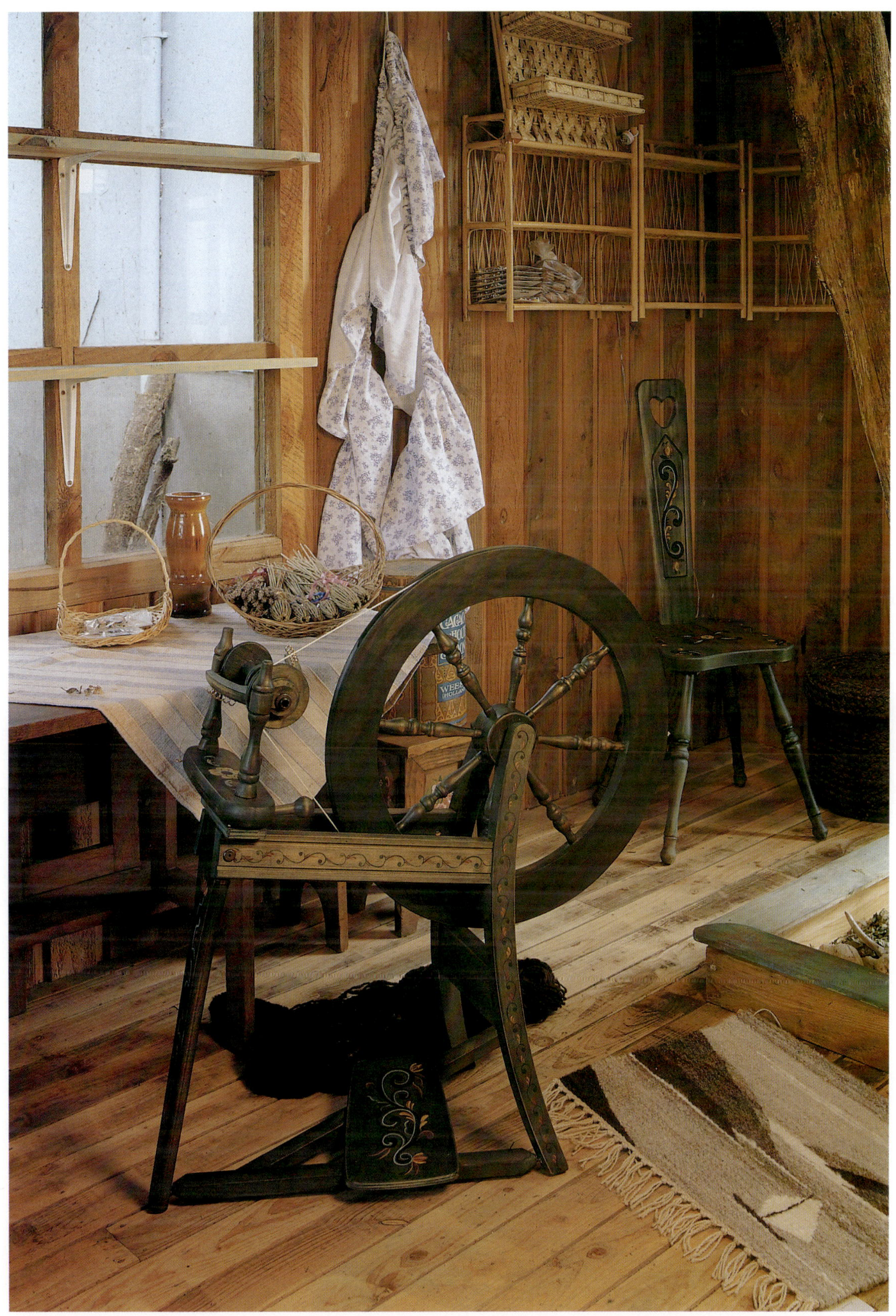

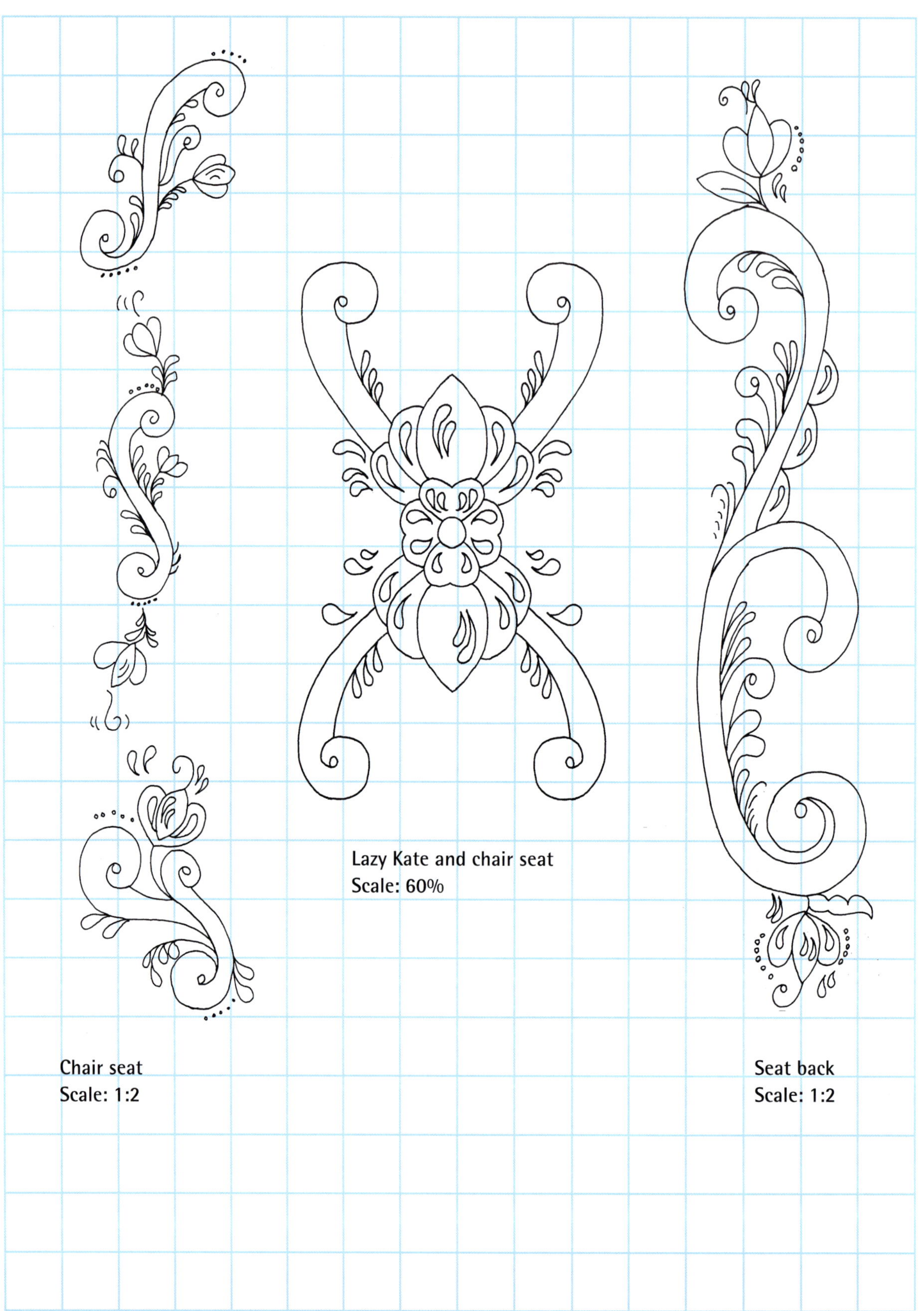

Lazy Kate and chair seat
Scale: 60%

Chair seat
Scale: 1:2

Seat back
Scale: 1:2

Seat

Scrolls: Teal Green.

Flowers: Burgundy and Yellow Oxide.

Line work: Carbon Black and Smoked Pearl.

Commas: A double load of Burgundy and Yellow Oxide.

Follow the instructions above for highlighting and shading.

The centre pattern is the same as the one for the Lazy Kate.

Legs

The turned parts of the legs are painted with Teal Green.

FINISHING

Varnish with two coats of polyurethane varnish using a No. 25 flat brush.

Assemble the spinning wheel and chair following the manufacturer's instructions. Sand back some of the painting to create a weathered look.

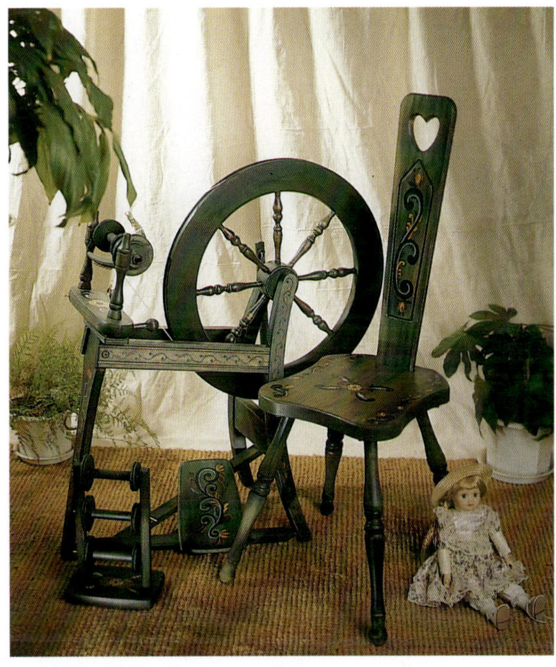

Enjoy these lovely pieces for years to come – not only to look at but to use as often as you wish for spinning beautiful New Zealand wool.

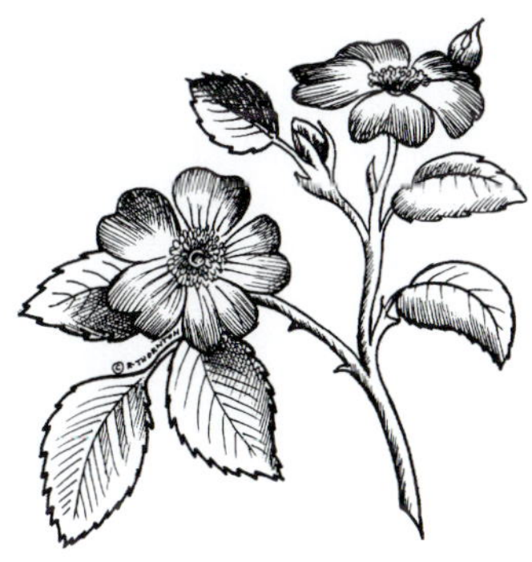

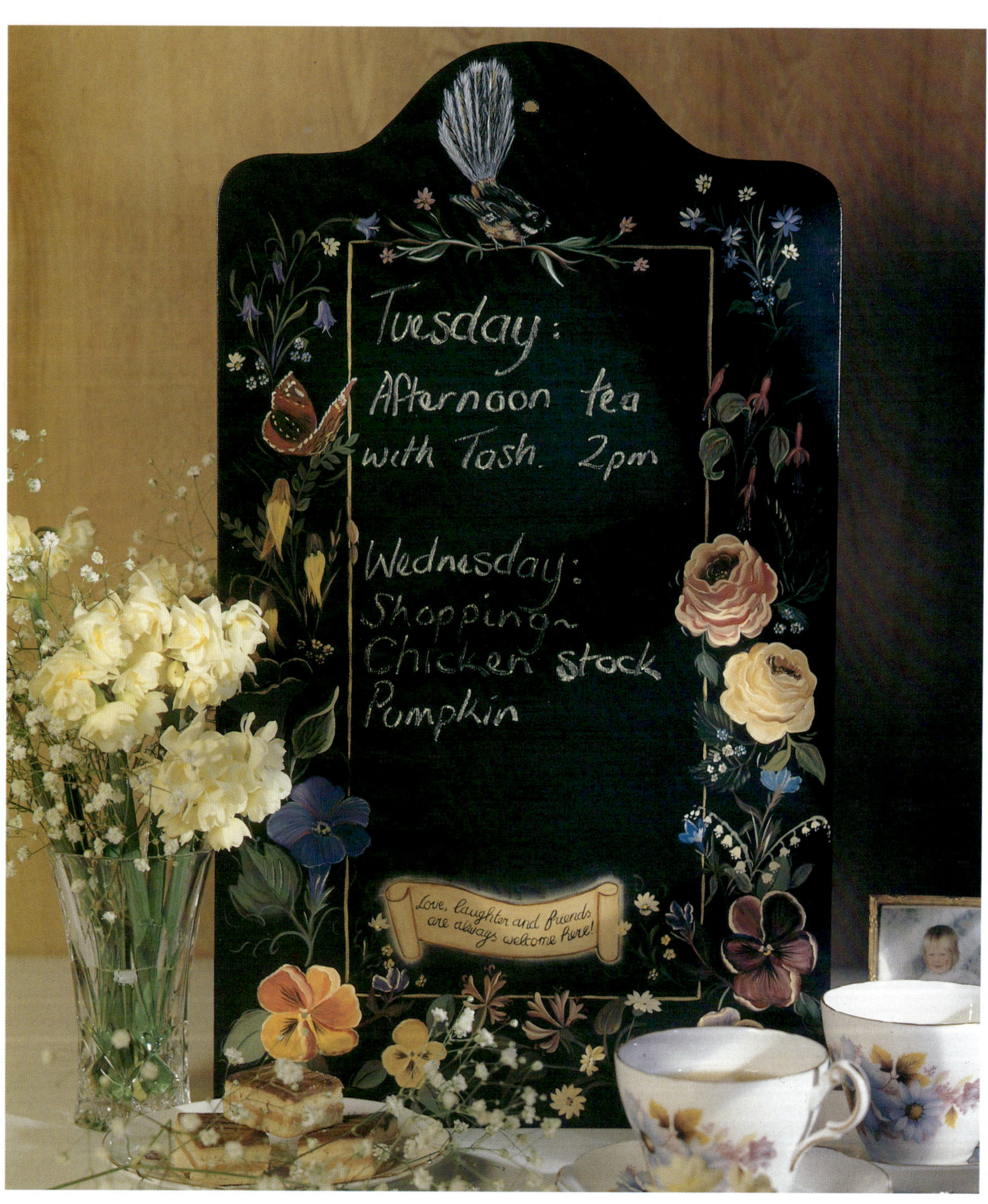
Tuesday:
Afternoon tea
with Tash. 2pm

Wednesday:
Shopping~
Chicken stock
Pumpkin

Love, laughter and friends
are always welcome here!

Blackboard with a Garland of Summer Flowers

I just love flowers; the colours and the shapes are a pleasure for the eye, not to mention the scents when you walk through the garden. Every time I plant and work in the garden I have a vision of how it will look one day – just flowers, flowers everywhere!

<table>
<tr><td>

Palette
Yellows: Yellow Oxide, Yellow Light
Brown: Brown Earth
Greens: Pine Green, Green Oxide, Antique Green
    (Matisse)
Reds: Burgundy, Napthol Crimson
Blue: Ultra Blue Deep
White: Warm White
Black: Carbon Black
Gold: Rich Gold
Purple: Diox. Purple
Orange: Norwegian Orange

</td><td>

Mediums
Jo Sonja Flow Medium
Burnt Umber oil paint
Artist's turpentine
Jo Sonja satin polyurethane varnish (oil-based)

Brushes
No. 25 basecoat brush
No. 3 round brush
No. 8 flat brush
No. 0 liner brush

</td></tr>
</table>

PREPARATION

Basecoat the board with three coats of Carbon Black, front and back. Sand lightly between coats.

Measure 6cm in from the edges of the board and pull a white chalk pencil line around the sides and top.

Trace on the pattern using white graphite paper. Place the fantail on top of the white chalk line (see photograph opposite).

PAINTING

Fantail

Basecoat lightly with watered-down Warm White.

Head and top of body

Basecoat top of body with Brown Earth. Basecoat head and breast with Norwegian Orange.

Make small strokes with Brown Earth and a little Carbon Black.

Overstroke with some Yellow Oxide and Warm White.

Wings

Fine strokes with Brown Earth, Carbon Black and Yellow Oxide. Use the liner brush.

Tail

Paint separate feathers with Carbon Black mixed with Warm White. Stroke in Carbon Black, Yellow Oxide and Warm White for more detail.

Eye

Carbon Black with a white dot.

Beak

Carbon Black highlighted with Warm White.

Legs

Warm White with a little Yellow Oxide.

Branch

A double load of Brown Earth and Warm White.

Leaves

Green Oxide highlighted with Warm White.

Flowers

Burgundy mixed with Warm White to a soft pink. The centre is a Burgundy dot.

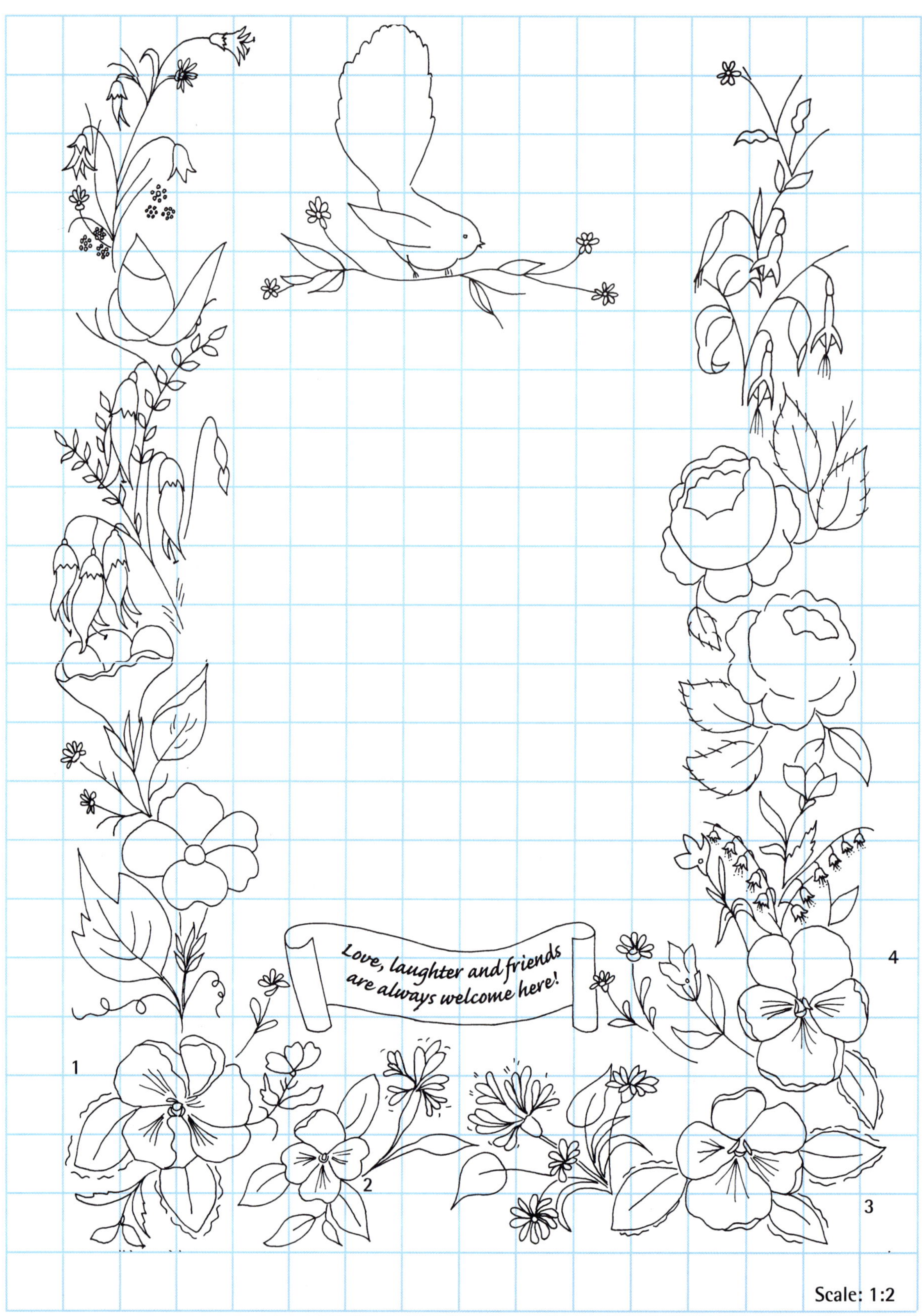

Love, laughter and friends
are always welcome here!
1
2
3
4
Scale: 1:2

Left side of the board

Bell flowers

Diox. Purple and Warm White double-loaded with a round brush, using little S strokes. Ultra Blue Deep can be picked up as well.

Leaves: Green Oxide with Yellow Oxide double-loaded with a round brush.

Butterfly

Basecoat with Burgundy.

Shade with a mix of Burgundy and Carbon Black.

Use Carbon Black and Warm White for line work.

Make little comma strokes around the butterfly with Warm White.

The body of the butterfly is painted with Rich Gold.

Kowhai

Stems: Green Oxide and Brown Earth double-loaded. Paint the stems first.

Leaves: Small strokes of Green Oxide. Veins are Brown Earth.

Buds: Brown Earth, highlighted with Warm White. Drybrush.

Flowers: Yellow Light, highlighted with Warm White.

Shade with Green Oxide.

Fine details in Pine Green. Drybrush.

Morning Glory

Basecoat with Ultra Blue Deep mixed with Warm White.

Pull strokes towards the centre with a load of Diox. Purple, Ultra Blue Deep and a little Napthol Crimson.

Divide the petals with a thin line of Napthol Crimson.

For turned edges double-load the brush with Ultra Deep Blue and Warm White and, with the white on the inside, pull around the top of the petals.

Paint dots in the centre with Yellow Oxide and Diox. Purple.

Line work with Diox. Purple.

Leaves: Green Oxide.

Shade with a mix of Diox. Purple and Pine Green.

Paint the veins with Diox. Purple.

Line work with Pine Green.

Pansy 1

(The pansies are numbered on the pattern from 1– 4)

Basecoat with Yellow Oxide.

Petal detail: Wash the centre of the petals – some with a little watery Burgundy and some with Norwegian Orange.

Double-load the brush with Yellow Oxide and Warm White and paint turned edges. Warm White can also be pulled down into the petals.

Veins: Paint with a mix of Diox. Purple and Carbon Black.

Paint a dot in the centre of the flower with Green Oxide.

Finish with two Warm White commas and one little Yellow Light comma.

Pansy 2

Basecoat with Yellow Oxide.

Wash with Yellow Light and Warm White.

Top of petal: Paint turned edges with Warm White turned into the petals.

Pansy 3

Basecoat with Ultra Blue Deep mixed with Warm White.

Wash with Diox. Purple and Ultra Blue Deep mixed with some Warm White.

Top of petal: Warm White.

Pansy 4

Basecoat with a mix of Burgundy and Ultra Blue Deep. Wash with Diox. Purple and in some petals a wash of Burgundy and Diox. Purple.

Top of petal: Warm White.

Leaves

Basecoat with Green Oxide.

Highlight with Antique Green while the Green Oxide is still wet.

Veins: Carbon Black.

Honeysuckle

Leaves: Pine Green

Shade with Burgundy or Yellow Oxide.

Flowers: Double-load a round brush with Napthol Crimson and Warm White to pull little commas. Each petal has two or three commas.

Paint little dots inside the petals using a liner brush or stylus.

Pull little strokes around the top of the petals with a liner brush.

Lobelia

Leaves: Brown Earth and Warm White.

Flowers: Ultra Blue Deep. Using a round brush, double-load with Warm White and pull down into the petals.

Lily of the Valley

Stems: Antique Green.

Flowers: Warm White.

Paint three little commas and dots at the end of each bell-shaped flower.

Roses (follow the worksheet)

Yellow Rose: Triple-loaded S strokes with Yellow Oxide, Warm White and Brown Earth. Centre: Brown Earth mixed with Carbon Black.

Red Rose: Double-loaded S strokes of Napthol Crimson and Warm White.

Leaves: Pine Green with line work in Antique Green.

Fuchsia (follow the worksheet)

Leaves: Green Oxide. Highlight with a little Green Oxide mixed with Warm White.

Veins: Burgundy

Flowers: Napthol Crimson and Diox. Purple; double-load the brush.

Drybrush with some Warm White on top.

The stamens are Diox. Purple.

Small flowers

Warm White, Ultra Blue Deep, Yellow Oxide. Use a stylus to make round dots.

Small daises

Warm White. Use Yellow Light to paint the centre of the flower with little commas with a yellow dot in the centre.

Scroll

Basecoat with Warm White.

Outline with Brown Earth.

Shade with Brown Earth using a side-loaded flat brush.

Lettering: Carbon Black.

ANTIQUING

Mix some Burnt Umber oil paint and artist's turpentine together on a small saucer until a creamy consistency (1:4). Using a lint-free cloth, rub some of this mixture onto the flowers to mellow the colours. Let dry for a couple of days.

FINISHING

Finish with two coats of polyurethane varnish (oil-based).

You can write on the blackboard using chalk or a chalk pencil. Wipe away with a damp cloth.

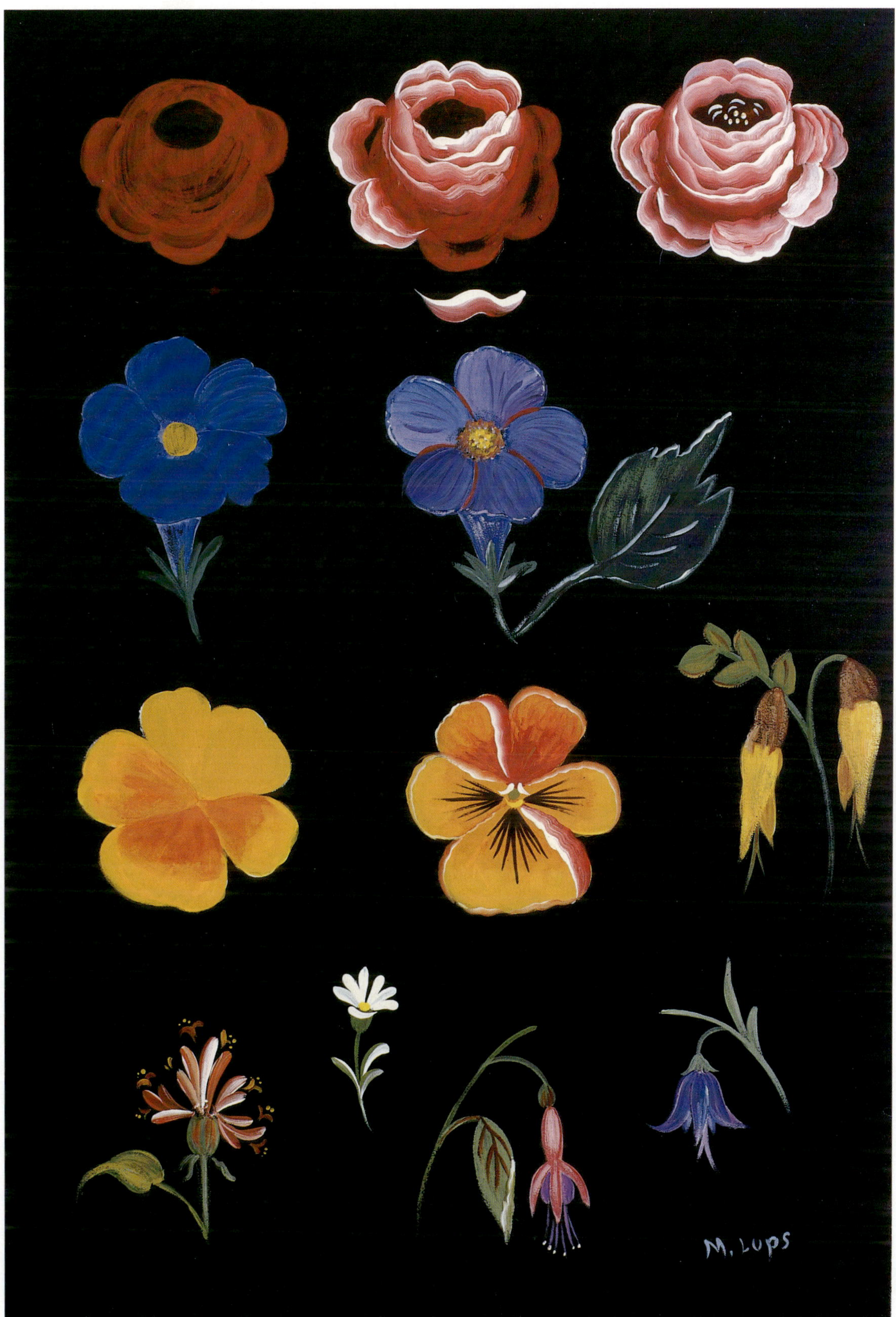

M. LUPS

Sunflower Petticoat Table

I've always loved sunflowers; they're so cheerful, bold and simple. I once saw a field full of them in France, nodding in the sun; it's an image that pops into my mind whenever I see them. To me they embody the warmth and vigour of summer. The first time I painted them I was on a watercolour painting course. The person taking the course arrrived one morning, arms filled with a huge bunch of brilliant, big-faced sunflowers. She put them into an equally huge vase and that was our study for the day.

They're not a complicated flower to paint so I thought they would be a good subject for my beginner folk art students to try. They were: everyone got good results. Of course you can paint them onto a variety of things; one of my students achieved great results when she painted them onto a T-shirt.

Palette
Yellows: Yellow Light, Yellow Oxide
Whites: Warm White, Soft White (background colour)
Greens: Pine Green, Teal Green
Black: Carbon Black
Orange: Norwegian Orange
Blue: Dolphin Blue (background colour)
Gold: Pale Gold
Browns: Burnt Umber, Brown Earth

Mediums
Jo Sonja Tannin Blocking Sealer for Wood
Jo Sonja Decor Crackle Medium
Jo Sonja Texture Paste
Jo Sonja satin polyurethane varnish (oil-based)

Brushes
No. 5 round brush
Liner brush
No. 25 soft varnish flat brush

PREPARATION

Seal the edges and legs of the table with Tannin Blocking Sealer. Let dry and sand well.

Basecoat the table top and legs with Soft White and sand well when dry; you should finish with a smooth surface.

Using a No. 25 flat brush, paint patches of Pale Gold onto the table top (concentrating on the centre) and legs.

When dry, brush on a nice thick layer of Decor Crackle Medium and leave until touch-dry.

Basecoat the table top and legs with Dolphin Blue; try to paint in the one direction with long even strokes.

Don't overstroke the Crackle Medium as that will cause it to lift off. The crackle appears straight away. Let dry and lightly apply another coat of Dolphin Blue. Let dry completely.

If necessary, sand any rough areas lightly.

Transfer the sunflowers onto the table using white graphite paper.

PAINTING

The drybrushing technique is used for all steps in this project.

Sunflowers

Basecoat the centres with Burnt Umber.

Basecoat the petals with Yellow Oxide.

Basecoat the leaves with Pine Green.

Petals

To create a sense of depth in the flower, drybrush the front petals with Warm White, painting two-thirds of the way down from the top of the petal towards the centre.

Drybrush the back petals with Norwegian Orange. Let dry.

Drybrush Yellow Light on all the petals, over the top of the first layer. This will soften the colours and create depth to your flowers.

Drybrush a little Yellow Oxide or Norwegian Orange out from the centre and down into the petals.

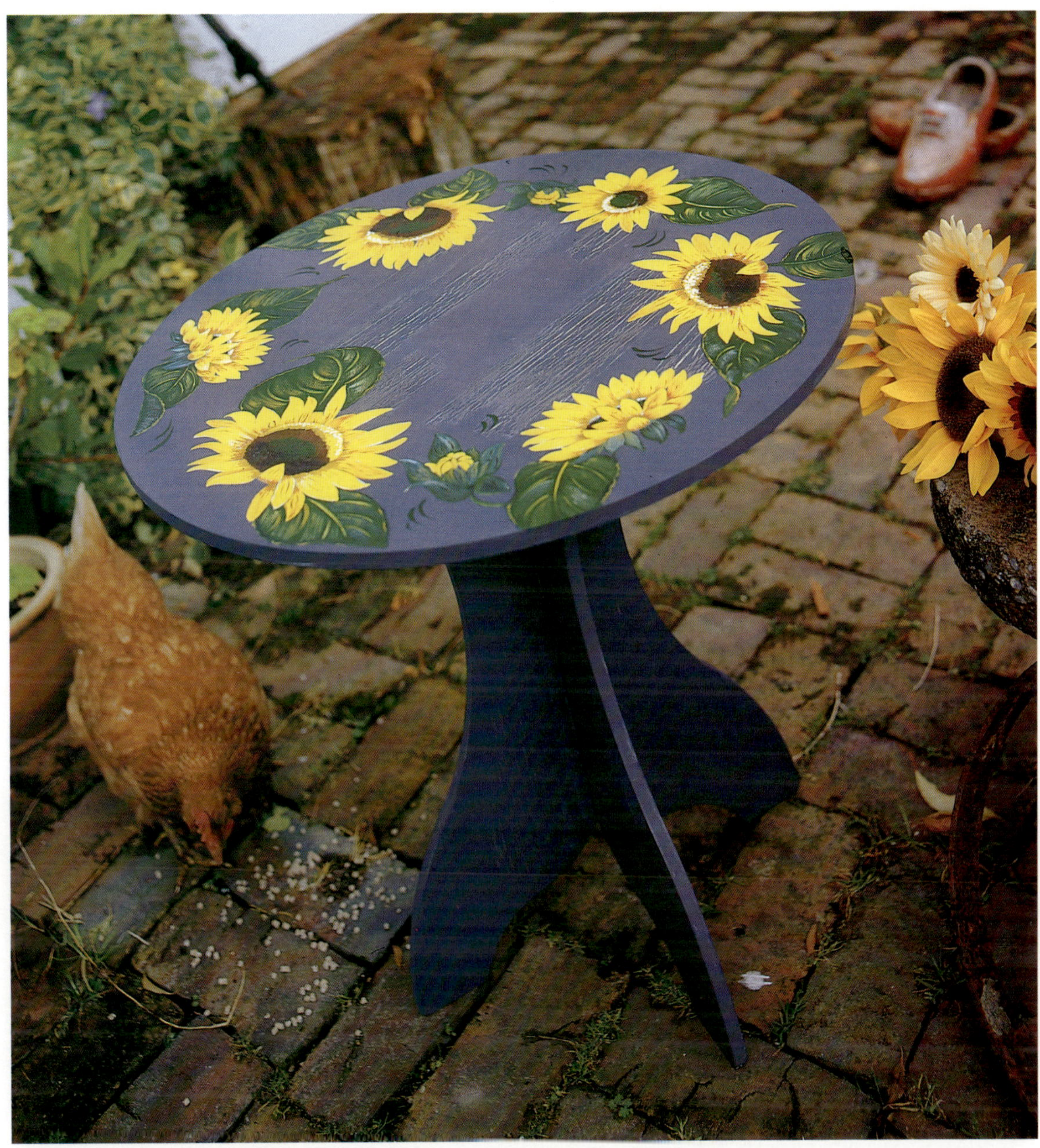

Use Brown Earth on a liner brush to add some fine line work in the petals.

Centres

Stipple the centre of the flowers using Brown Earth on a round brush.

Lightly stipple Yellow Oxide on the top half of the flower, on whichever side you want the light to fall. Let the colour fade out towards the opposite side.

Pick up a little Yellow Light and stipple this on top of the Yellow Oxide.

Stipple a little Warm White on top of that layer.

Stipple Carbon Black on the bottom half of the flower's centre, to create a shadow, fading it out towards the top.

Stipple Pine Green in the centre of the sunflower.

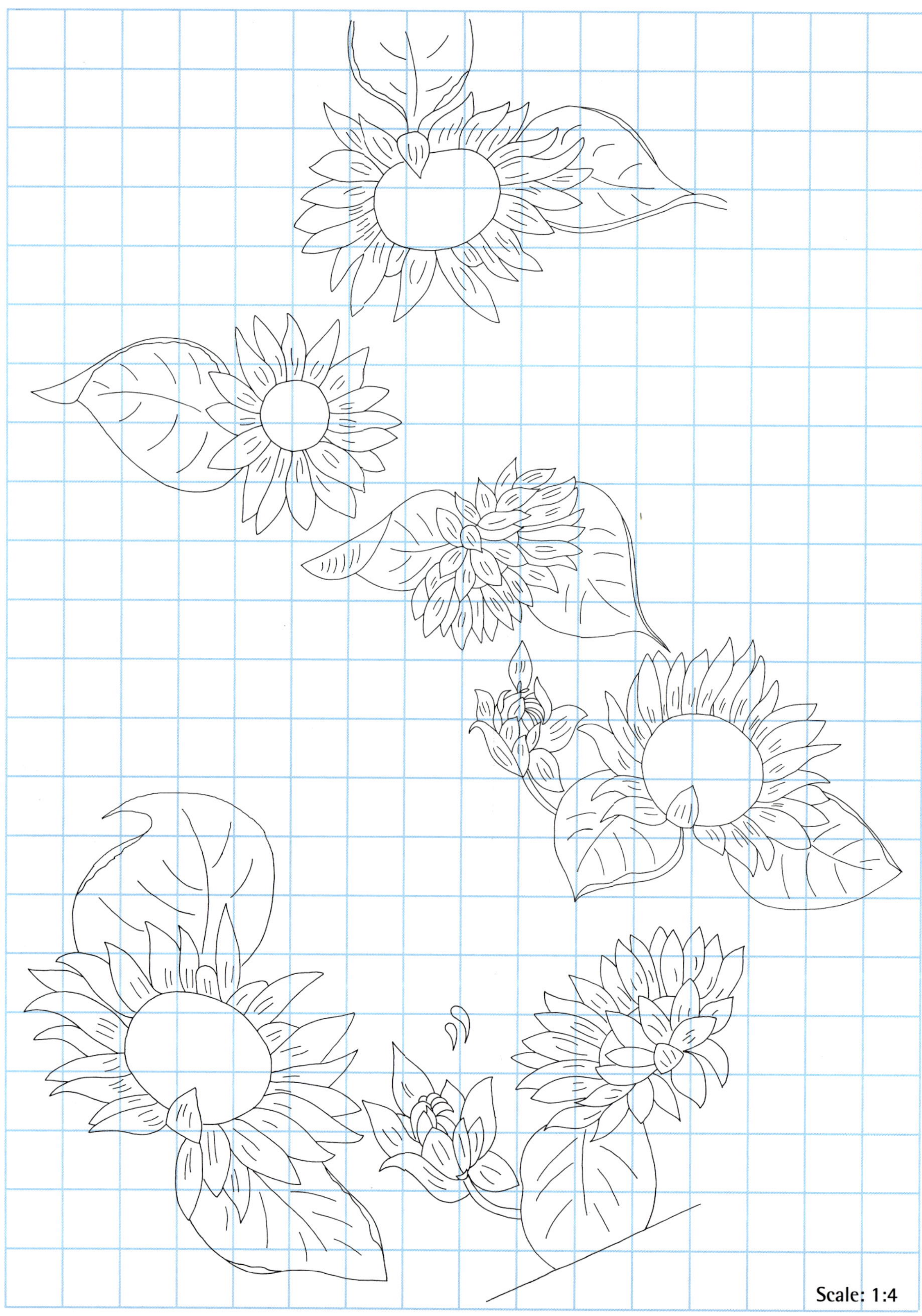

Scale: 1:4

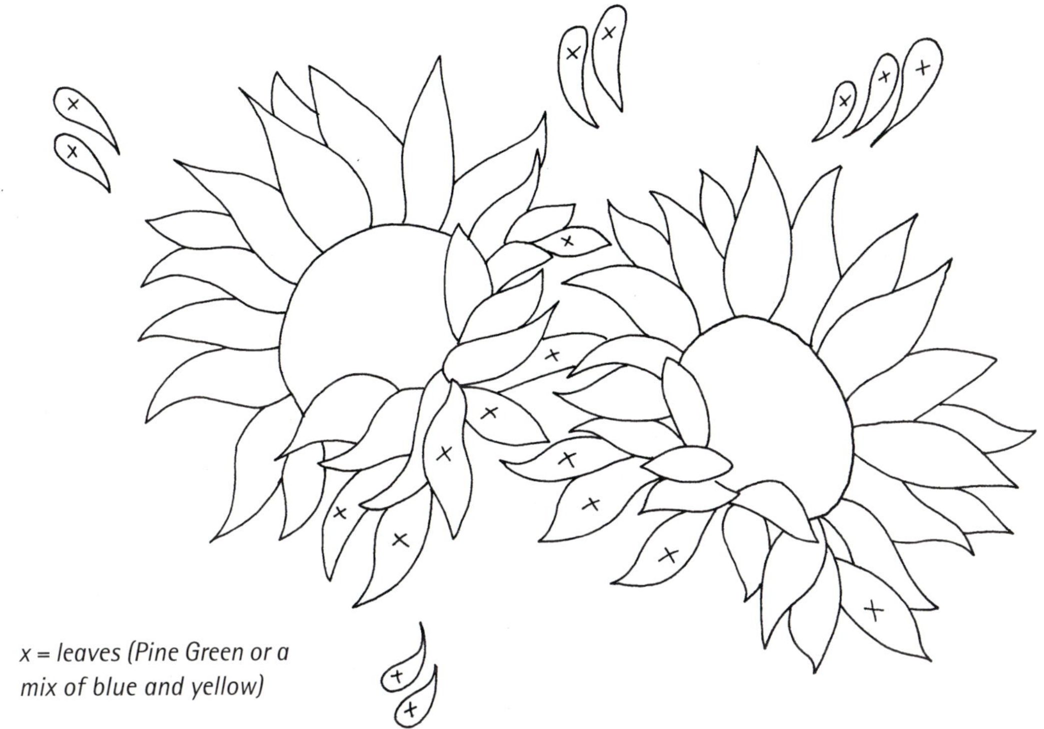

*x = leaves (Pine Green or a
mix of blue and yellow)*

Jo Sonia colours: basecoat

Burnt Umber centre

Yellow Oxide petals

Pine Green leaves

*Basecoat the
sunflowers*

*Drybrush light colours on
top of petals. Skim over
the surface, no water.
Build up layers.*

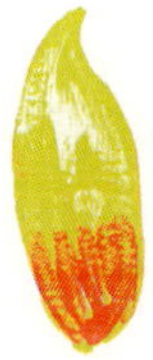

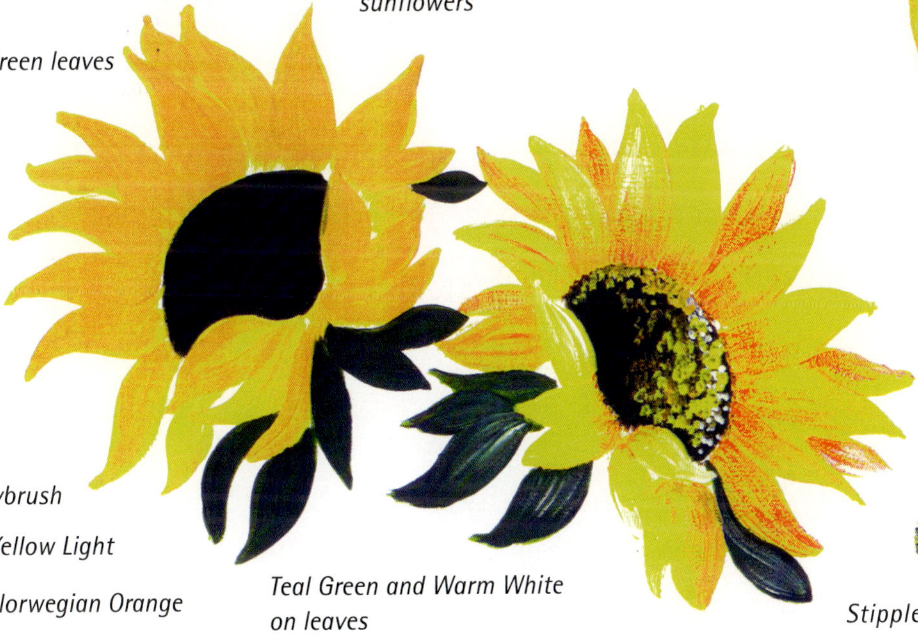

Colours: drybrush

Yellow Light

Norwegian Orange

Warm white

Teal green

*Teal Green and Warm White
on leaves*

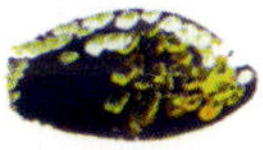

*Stipple the centre
with lighter colours*

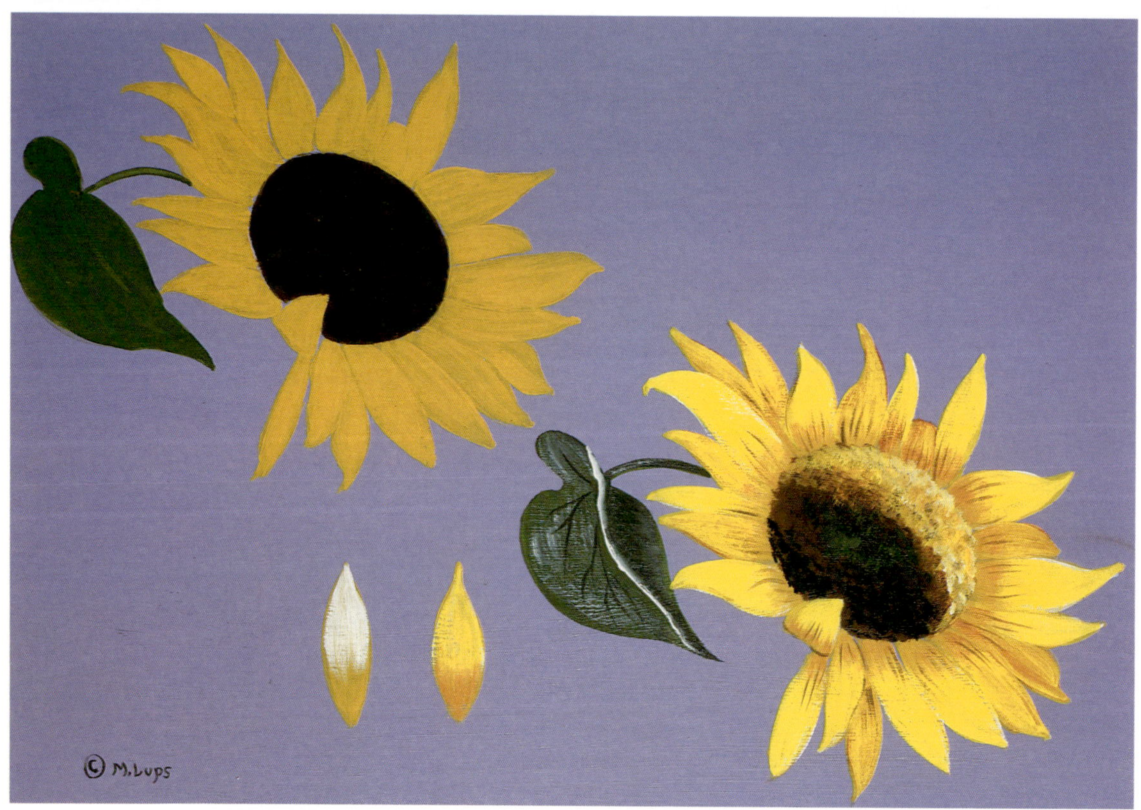

Leaves

Paint the veins with Yellow Light. Drybrush Yellow Oxide or Warm White mixed with Teal Green between the veins.

Turned edges are a double load of Pine Green and Yellow Oxide.

Outline the leaves using Yellow Oxide on a liner brush.

VARNISHING

The table is varnished with oil-based polyurethane varnish. Two or three coats are needed for a durable finish. Let it cure for a week before using.

Bears for Christmas

I have always loved bears. They remind me of cuddles at night just before bedtime. My bear was humble; just a tiny little thing I got from 'Sint Nicolaas', the Dutch Santa Claus, when I was a young girl. I loved him for years, together with my dolls, until one day I lost him and never saw him again. Maybe that is why I paint bears now.

The tree is for my children. Every year we put up our Teddy Christmas Bear Tree and light the tiny candles. I hope you enjoy painting this project. Perhaps the work will bring you happy memories of past Christmases and bears you have loved.

The tree is the Ashford Kiwi Christmas Tree.

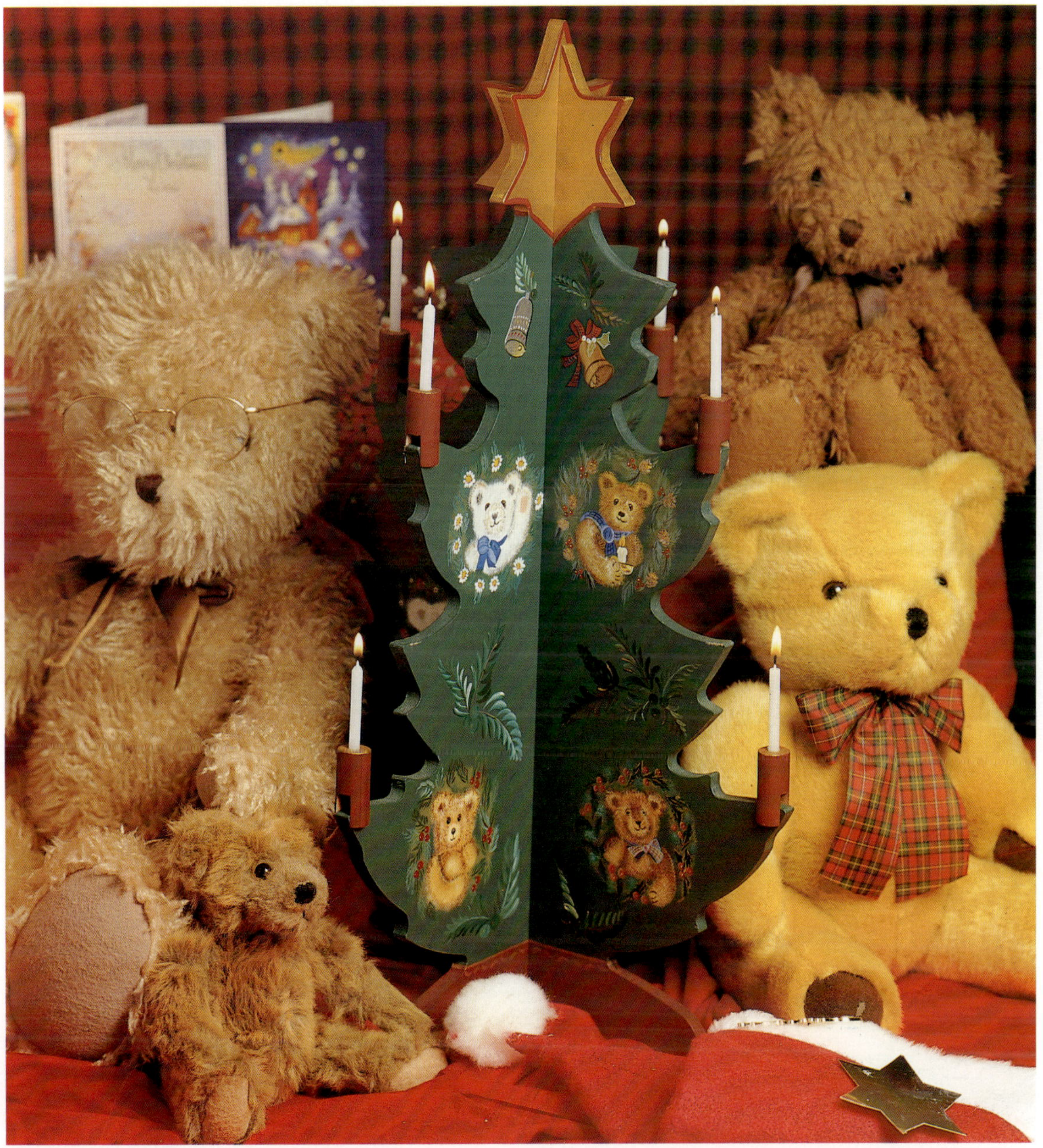

Palette

White: Warm White
Grey: Nimbus Grey
Brown: Brown Earth, Burnt Umber
Black: Carbon Black
Yellows: Yellow Light, Yellow Oxide, Raw Sienna
Reds: Napthol Crimson, Burgundy, Indian Red Oxide
Blue: Cobalt Blue Hue
Purple: Diox. Purple
Greens: Pine Green, Green Oxide, Pthalo Green
Gold: Rich Gold

Mediums

Jo Sonja Tannin Blocking Sealer
Jo Sonja satin polyurethane varnish (water-based)
Jo Sonja Clear Glazing Medium

Brushes

No. 3 round brush
No. 0 liner brush
No. 8 flat brush
1/4-inch comb/rake brush
1/4-inch deerfoot brush
flat basecoating brush

PREPARATION

Sand the tree lightly with sandpaper. The edges of the tree are rough – to get a smooth finish seal the edges with Tannin Blocking Sealer before basecoating.

Basecoat the main part of the tree with a least two coats of Pine Green and use Rich Gold for the star. Use Indian Red Oxide for the base and the candle cups.

Mix a little Clear Glazing Medium with your basecoat (1:3). This will make basecoating much easier and produce a smoother finish. I usually basecoat my pieces the day before the decorating, to allow the paint to cure.

When dry, transfer the pattern with white graphite paper. When placing your pattern, take care to avoid the central vertical line of the tree as this will not be visible when the two parts of the tree are put together.

PAINTING

Bears

General

Basecoat the bears first, then let dry. After basecoating, stipple each bear all over with the basecoat using the deerfoot brush to make it fluffy.

Stipple the darker areas, inside ears, around snout and outside arms with the deerfoot brush.

Use the comb brush to highlight the bear, especially around the top of the ears, the snout, inside the arms and on the tummy.

Eyes and nose are painted with Carbon Black or Brown Earth and Carbon Black. Paws are painted in Napthol Crimson mixed with Warm White.

White bears

Basecoat with Warm White. Stipple to make the bear fluffy.

Shade with Nimbus Grey or Brown Earth, then highlight with Warm White, stippling the colours to add texture.

Yellow bears

Basecoat with Yellow Oxide. Stipple.

Shade with Brown Earth mixed with Raw Sienna, then highlight with Warm White, stippling the colours to add texture.

Brown bears

Basecoat with Brown Earth mixed with Warm White. Stipple.

Shade with Burnt Umber, then highlight with Warm White or Brown Earth mixed with Warm White, stippling the colours to add texture.

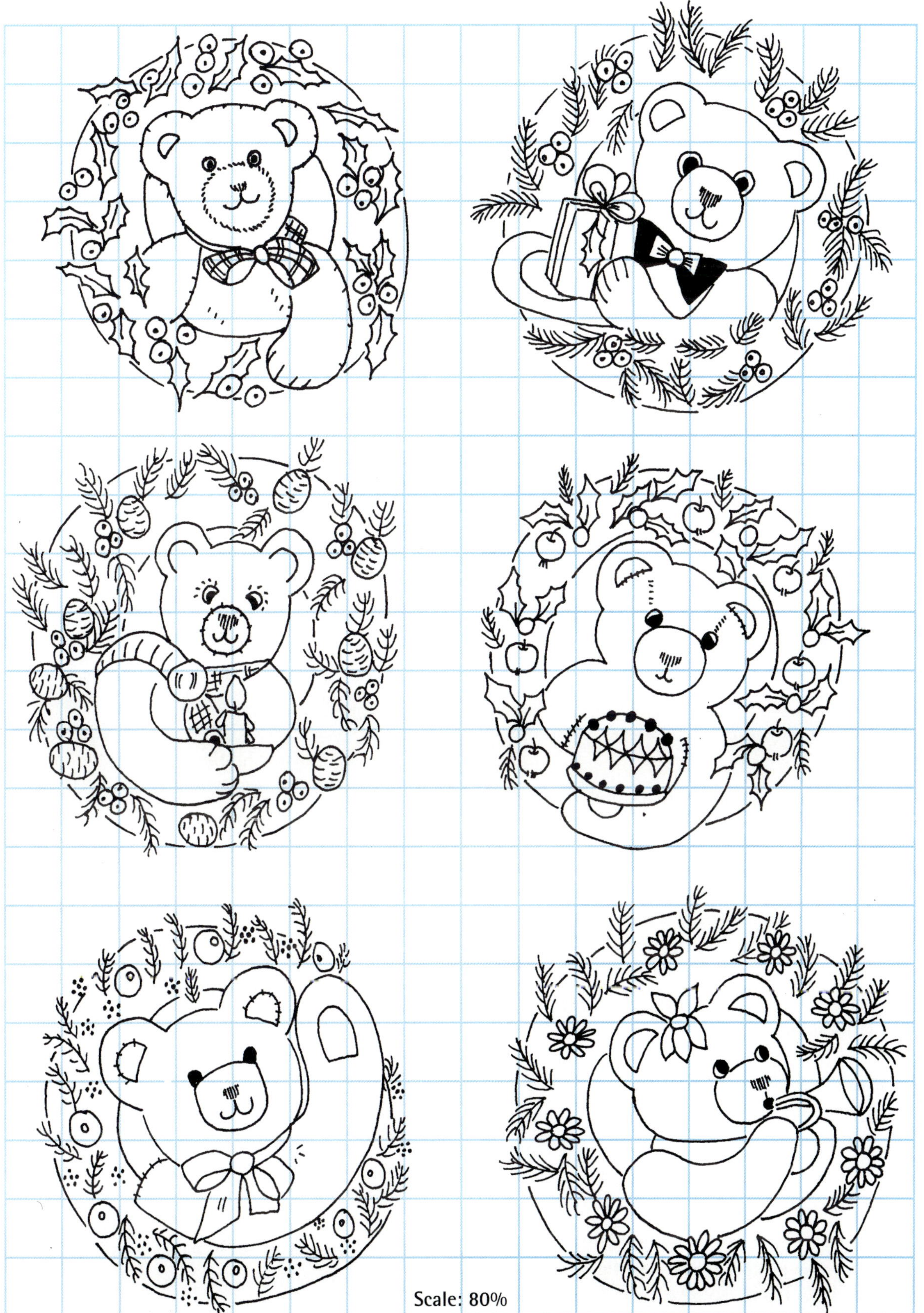

Scale: 80%

Detail for Bears (follow the worksheet opposite)

Dark red bow
Basecoat with Burgundy.
Highlight with Burgundy mixed with Warm White.
Outline with Carbon Black.

Light blue bow
Basecoat with Cobalt Blue Hue.
Highlight Cobalt Blue Hue mixed with Warm White.

Blue plaid bow
Basecoat with Cobalt Blue Hue.
Shade with Cobalt Blue Hue mixed with Carbon Black.
Highlight with Warm White.
Plaid with Napthol Crimson, Green Oxide.

Red plaid bow
Basecoat with Napthol Crimson.
Shade with Pine Green inside the bow.
Plaid with Pine Green and Warm White.

Bow tie
Paint the collar with Carbon Black.
Paint the tie with Warm White.
Paint details with Carbon Black and Warm White mixed to a grey.

Scarf
Basecoat with Cobalt Blue Hue.
Highlight with Cobalt Blue Hue mixed with Warm White.
Paint linework with Cobalt Blue Hue mixed with Carbon Black.

Cakes
Basecoat with Warm White or Warm White mixed with Yellow Oxide.
Berries: Napthol Crimson with a little gold dot just off-centre.
Holly leaves: Pine Green outlined with Red Gold.
Icing: Use an old fuzzy brush and stipple thick Warm White on top of the cake.

Red parcel
Basecoat with Warm White. Use a flat brush and side-load with Napthol Crimson around the sides.
Bow: Napthol Crimson.
Dots: Green Oxide.

Purple parcel
Basecoat with Warm White. Use a flat brush and side-load with Yellow Oxide around the sides.
Bow: Diox. Purple.
Paint linework with a mix of Diox. Purple and Warm White.

Trumpets
Basecoat with Yellow Oxide, then paint again with Rich Gold.
Outline with Burnt Umber.

Candle and holder
Basecoat with Warm White.
Paint details with Yellow Oxide, Carbon Black.
Use Napthol Crimson, thinned down, for the flame.

Wreaths (follow the worksheet)
Using the deerfoot brush, stipple the wreaths lightly with Green Oxide. Work on one side of the tree at a time.

Holly leaves
Pine Green outlined with Rich Gold.

Berries
Napthol Crimson, outlined with Rich Gold.
Carbon Black dot just off-centre.

Needles
Pthalo Green mixed with Warm White. Pine Green mixed with Warm White.

Roses
Basecoat with Burgundy. Overstroke with Napthol Crimson using comma strokes.
Dots are Warm White.

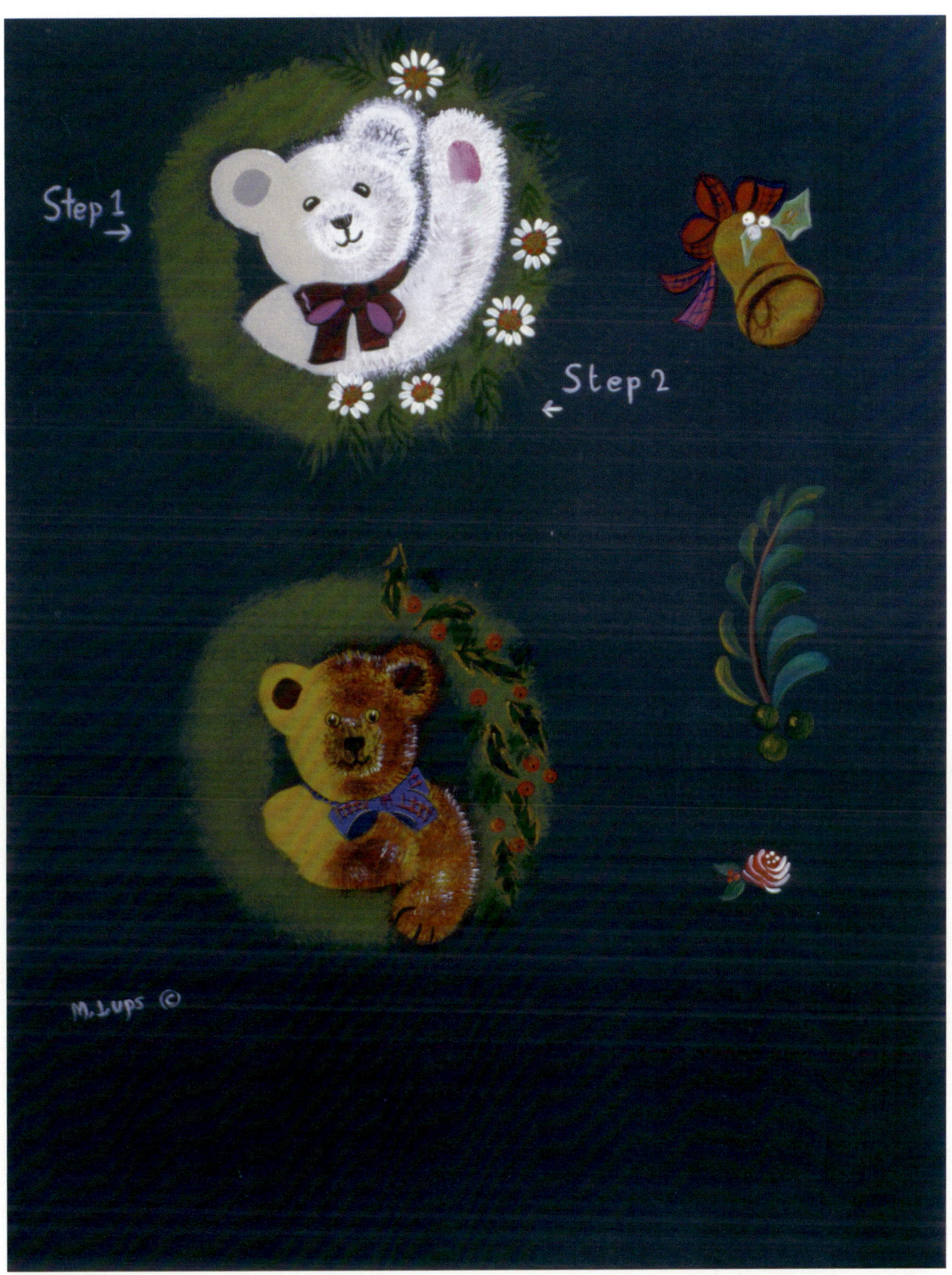
Step 1
Step 2
M. Lups ©

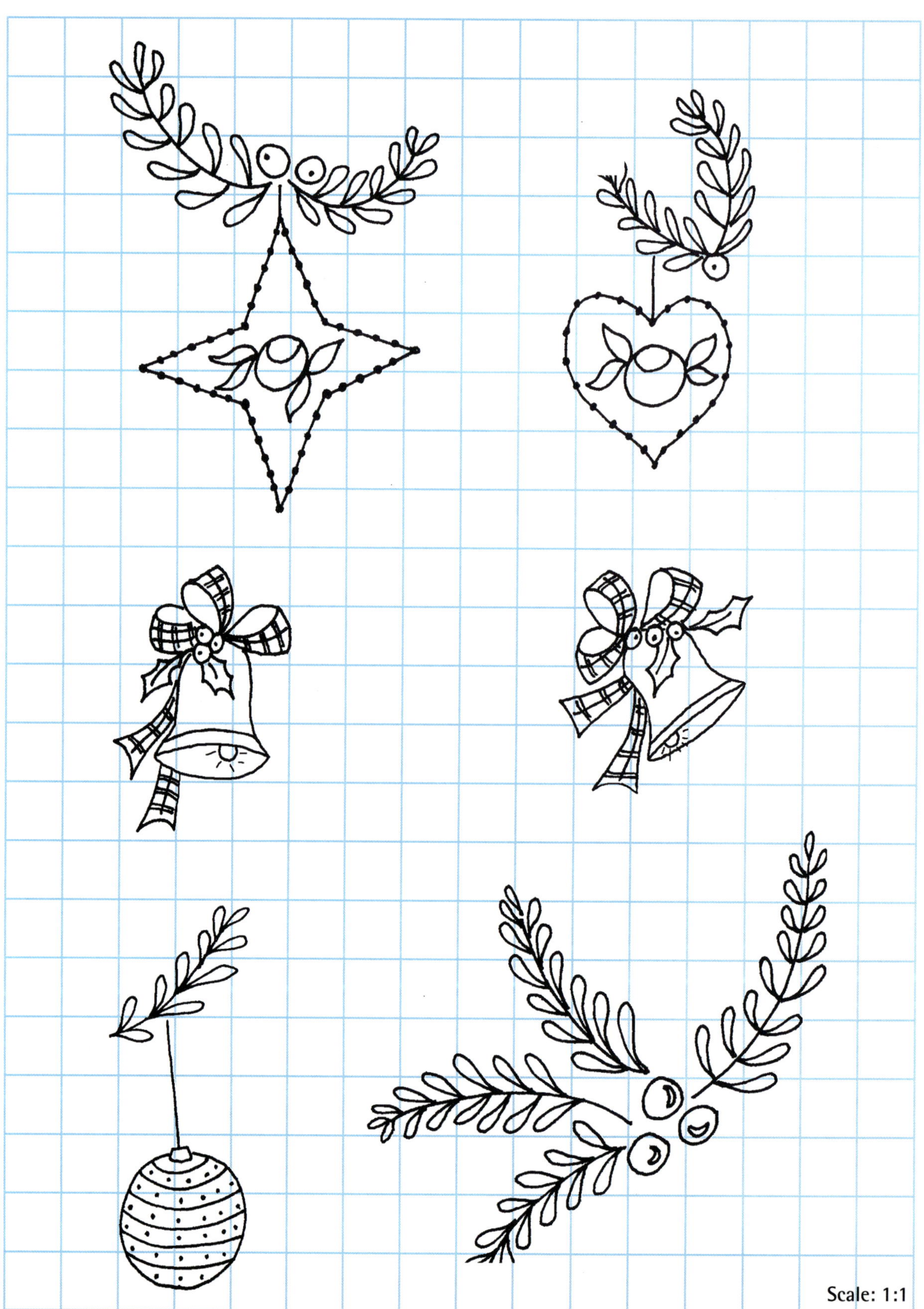

Scale: 1:1

Daisies

Paint the centre with Yellow Oxide.

Make comma strokes with Warm White.

Pinecones

Make small comma strokes with Brown Earth mixed with Warm White.

Apples

Napthol Crimson. Details in Brown Earth.

Tree Decorations

Star, heart

Basecoat with Yellow Oxide.

Second basecoat with Rich Gold.

Rose is Napthol Crimson.

Commas with Warm White and Napthol Crimson mixed with Warm White.

Dots are Napthol Green.

Round decorations

Basecoat with Warm White or Yellow Oxide.

Outline with Napthol Green.

Dots are Rich Gold.

Christmas Bells

Basecoat with Yellow Oxide.

Second basecoat with Rich Gold.

Highlight with Warm White.

Outline with Burnt Umber.

Bow: Napthol Green.

Plaid ribbon: Cobalt Blue Hue and Rich Gold.

Sprigs

Branches: Brown Earth.

Leaves: Comma strokes double-loaded with Pthalo Green, Pine Green and Rich Gold.

Berries

Pine Green with Pthalo Green or Napthol Crimson.

Gold stroke off-centre.

Base

Paint line work and commas with Rich Gold.

Top star

Outline with Burgundy.

FINISHING

Erase all graphite lines after you finish painting.

Varnish with two or three coats of water-based polyurethane varnish.

Sand lightly between coats with a fine sandpaper.

Paste wax if desired.

Enjoy your tree for many Christmases to come!

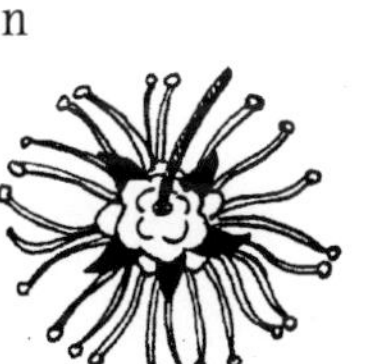

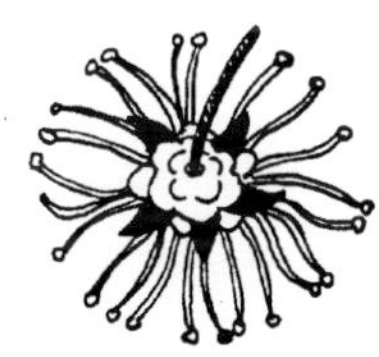

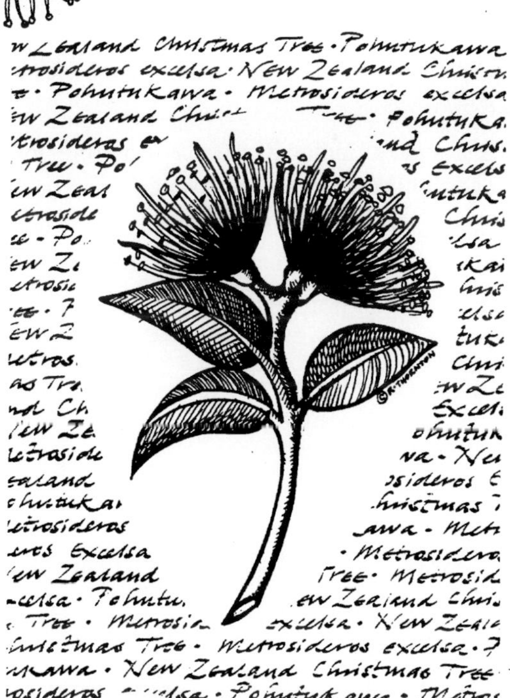

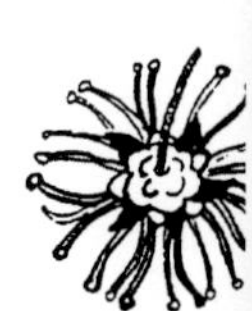

Rocking Horse

When I first saw this rocking horse I immediately had a picture in my mind of an old well-loved rocking horse – perhaps tucked away in the attic – that once found evokes all the good memories of a childhood past.

I hope I have achieved this impression by using only a few primary colours, and antiquing and rubbing away the paint. I hope you enjoy painting this piece for the child in your life.

Palette
Reds: Indian Red Oxide, Burgundy
White: Smoked Pearl
Black: Carbon Black

Mediums
Burnt Umber oil paint

Artist's turpentine
Jo Sonja satin polyurethane varnish (oil-based)
Jo Sonja Crackle medium

Brushes
No. 8 flat brush
No. 3 round brush
No. 25 flat brush for varnishing

PREPARATION

Sand all the pieces very well with fine sandpaper.

Use a tackcloth to remove the dust.

PAINTING

Base

Make a wash of Indian Red Oxide, watering down the paint on a saucer (5 parts water: 1 part paint).

Use a soft No. 25 flat brush and paint this water mixture onto all the base parts. Let dry.

Sand lightly and if necessary apply a second coat.

Frame

Make a wash of Carbon Black. Apply this to the framework as above.

Horse

Make a wash of Smoked Pearl and apply as above.

Eyes: Carbon Black, one each side.

Nostrils: Burgundy, one each side.

Spots: Carbon Black mixed with Smoked Pearl. Apply with a sea sponge, keeping the effect light and airy. Let dry.

Handholds: Burgundy.

Saddle

Create a saddle about 15cm wide by painting with Carbon Black. Outline with Burgundy.

Bridle

Refer to the photograph and draw in the bridle (about 1cm wide) with pencil. It doesn't matter if the lines are not perfect – this adds to the old worn look. Burgundy. Outline with Carbon Black.

FINISHING

Assemble the horse following the manufacturer's instructions.

With sandpaper No. 220, sand away the paint to create a worn look, especially where the horse would have been handled a lot, i.e. the base, saddle, handle and head.

Lastly, antique with Burnt Umber oil paint mixed with artist's turpentine and rub on this antiquing medium, particularly to the legs, head handle.

Let dry for at least a week before varnishing with three coats of oil-based polyurethane varnish.

Ready for play!

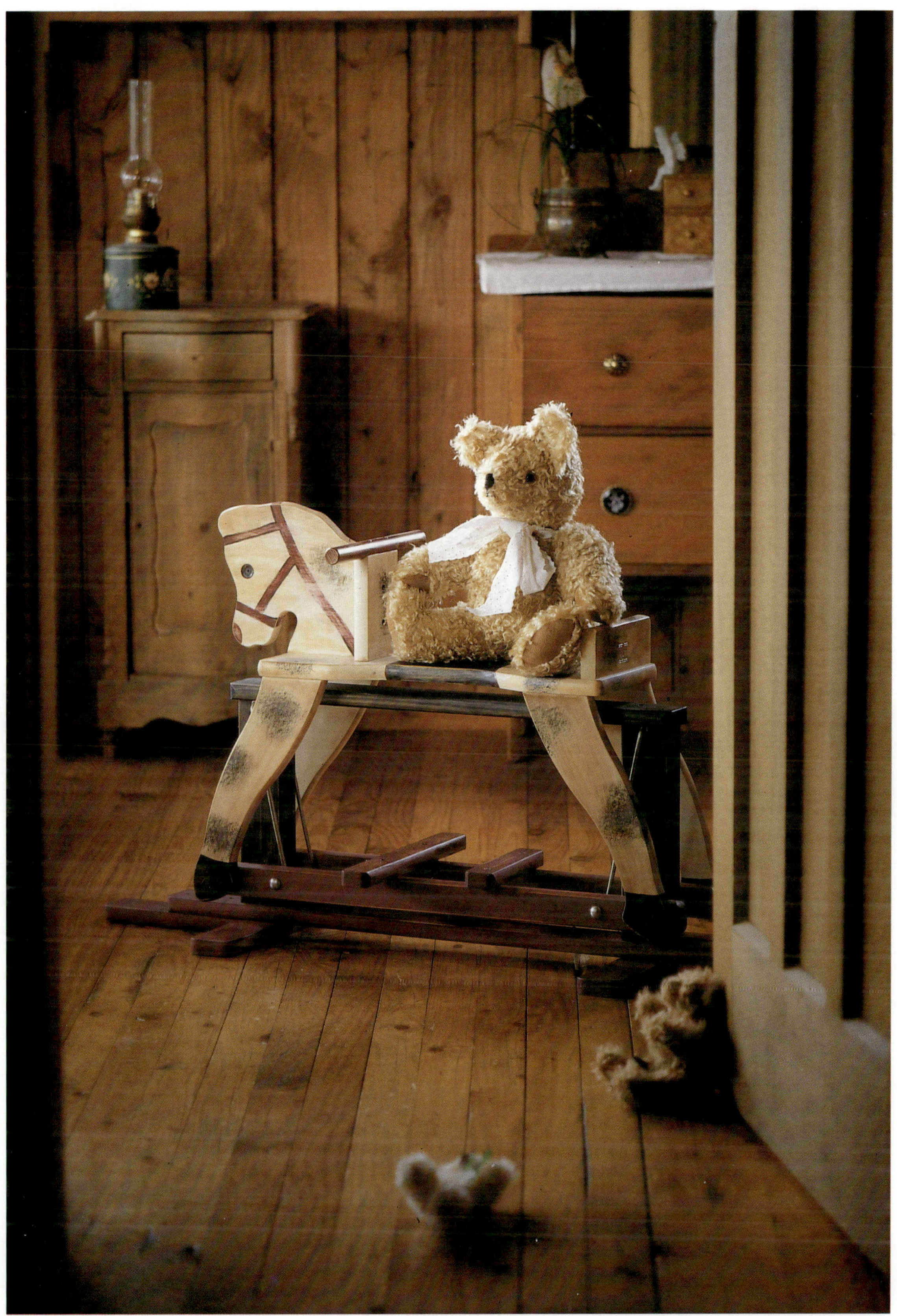

Goldminer's Cottage on Flower Press

On the West Coast of New Zealand there are many cottages like this, which date back to the goldmining days of the 1800s when miners travelled from distant places around the world to seek their fortune.

Very small and simple, they form quite a contrast to the modern homes of today. I painted the mountain daisy around it, a wild flower found among the mountain vegetation of New Zealand.

<table>
<tr><td>

Palette
Yellows: Yellow Oxide, Yellow Light
Whites: Warm White, Smoked Pearl
Greens: Pine Green, Green Oxide
Black: Carbon Black
Blue: Azure (background paint)
Browns: Brown Earth, Burnt Umber, Fawn
Red: Burgundy

</td><td>

Mediums
Jo Sonja Decor Crackle Medium
Burnt Umber oil paint
Artist's turpentine
Jo Sonja satin polyurethane varnish (oil-based)

</td></tr>
</table>

PREPARATION

Basecoat the flower press on all sides with Azure background paint. Sand lightly.

Apply another coat of Azure.

Transfer the pattern using white graphite paper.

PAINTING

Goldminer's Cottage

Basecoat the roof with Smoked Pearl using a No. 3 round brush.

Basecoat the walls with Fawn.

Basecoat the door with Burgundy.

Basecoat the window with Burnt Umber.

Basecoat the chimney with Burnt Umber.

Roof

Drybrush to build up about three layers of Smoked Pearl to create the look of a weathered roof.

Pull fine line work down with Brown Earth on a liner brush.

Create the corrugated iron roof with little black strokes.

Walls

Double-load a round brush with Warm White and paint small uneven strokes, and also create the brick wall.

Bricks: Brown Earth and Yellow Oxide.

Drybrush a little Brown Earth or Carbon Black in between the bricks.

Door

With Burnt Umber on a liner brush, pull lines down from top to bottom.

Drybrush a little Yellow Oxide in between lines.

Window

Shade with Yellow Oxide on one side.

Chimney

Little strokes of Yellow Oxide.

Posts

Burnt Umber.

Finish with Carbon Black floated under the roof, around the door and on top of the roof.

Hedges

Stipple with Pine Green using a deerfoot brush.

Stipple a second coat with Yellow Oxide and Carbon Black.

Stipple a third coat with Pine Green and Yellow Oxide.

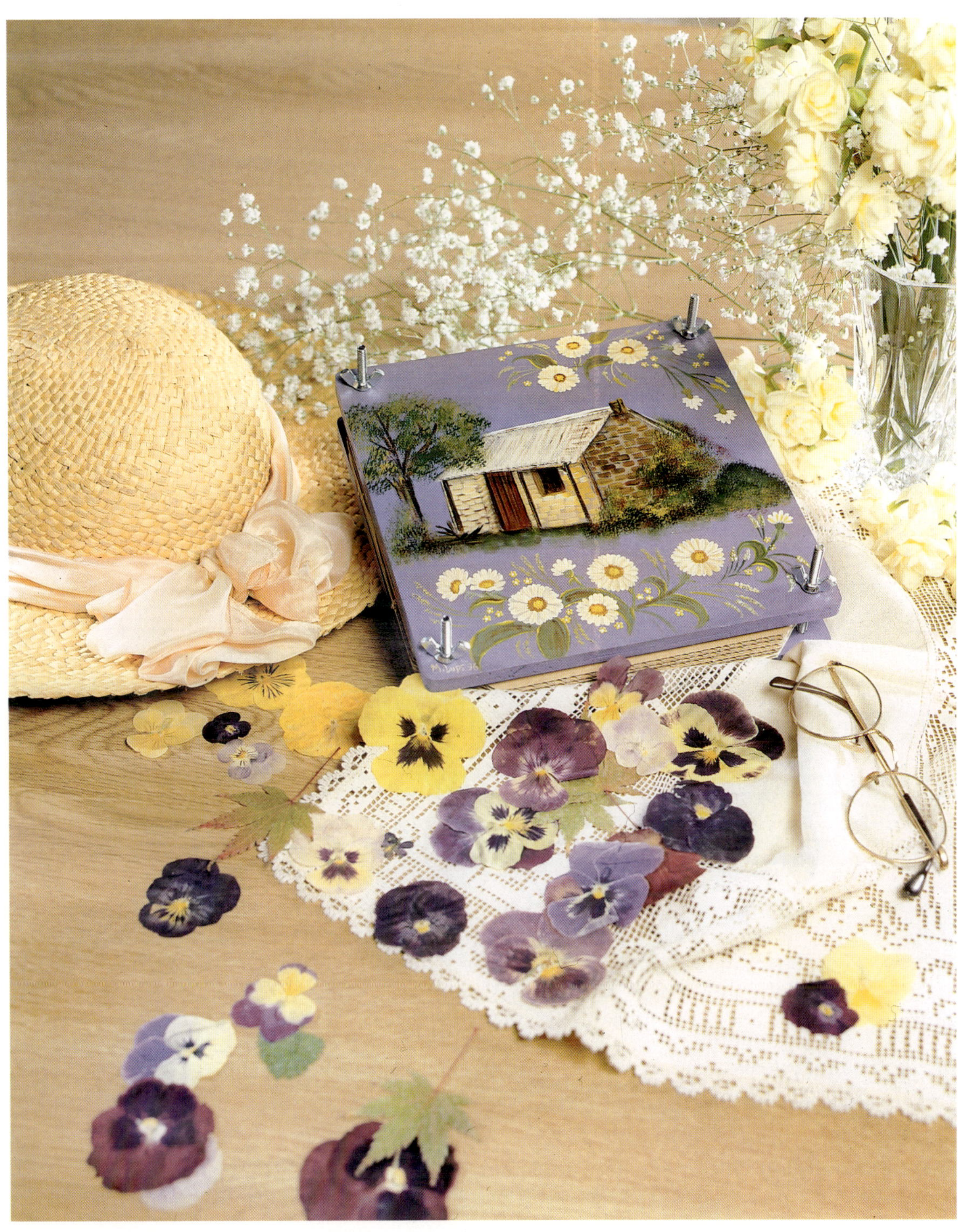

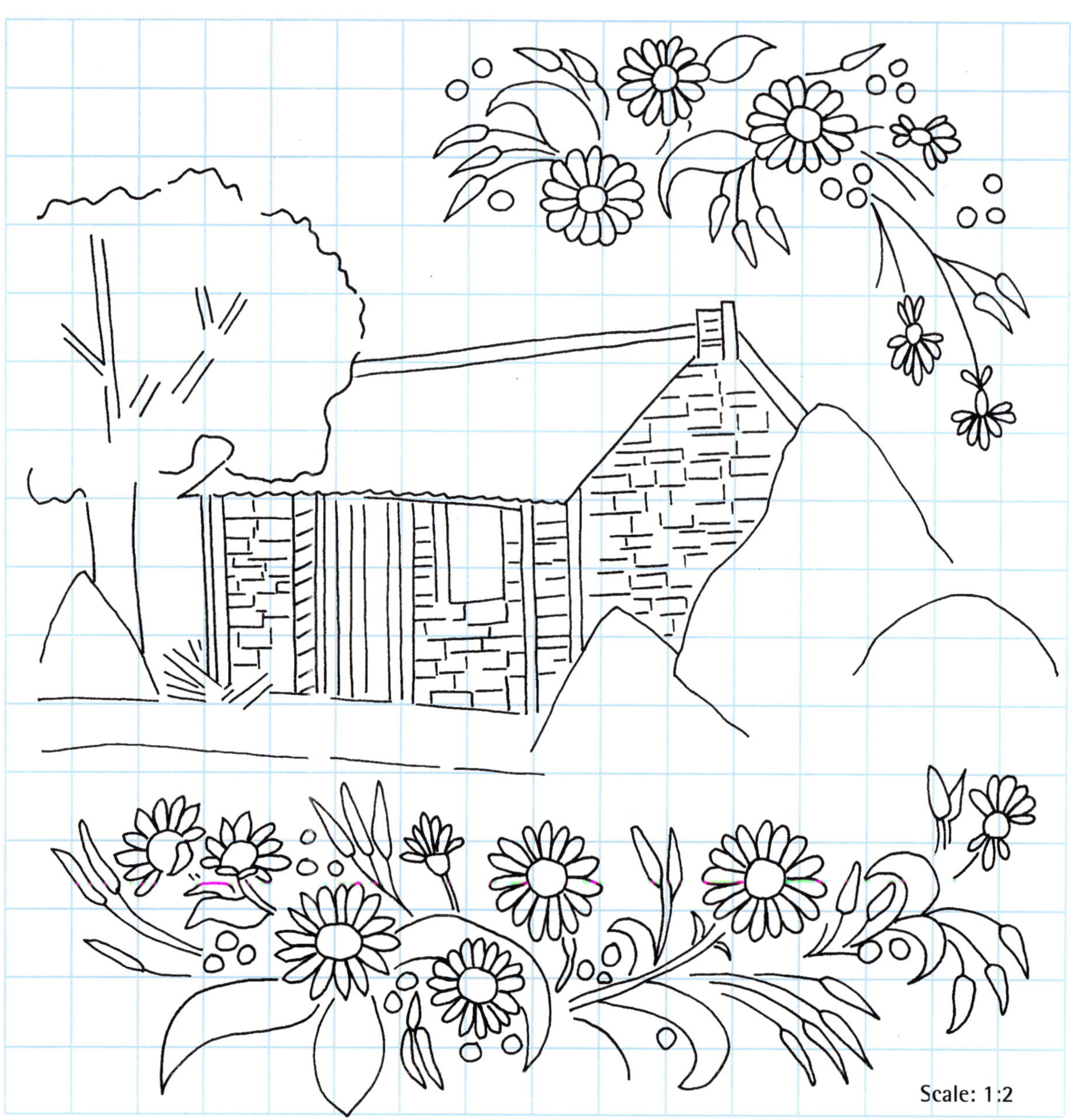

Tree Trunk

Drybrush with Brown Earth and Carbon Black.

The rest of the tree is stippled with Pine Green and
Yellow Oxide.

Finish with a float of Pine Green under the door
and walls.

Mountain Daisies

Leaves

Basecoat with Pine Green.

Drybrush a little Brown Earth in the centre.

Pull Yellow Light around the edges.

Daisies

Yellow Oxide in the centre.

Stipple a little Brown Earth around the centre.

Petals are teardrop strokes with Warm White and
Yellow Oxide. Let dry.

Overstroke with Warm White, using enough paint
on the brush to make the flowers look textured.

Dot Flowers

Little dots with Yellow Light, using a stylus.

FINISHING

Paint Crackle Medium on top of the daisies. Let dry.

Rub a little antiquing medium (Burnt Umber oil paint mixed with artist's turpentine 1:4) onto the flowers, to enhance the crackled effect.

The back of the flower press is sponged with Pine Green, then a second coat with Yellow Oxide and a third coat with a little Burgundy.

Use a sea sponge and dab the paint on your palette first before applying it to the surface of the flower press – you want to create a soft muted look.

Let dry and varnish with two coats of oil-based polyurethane varnish.

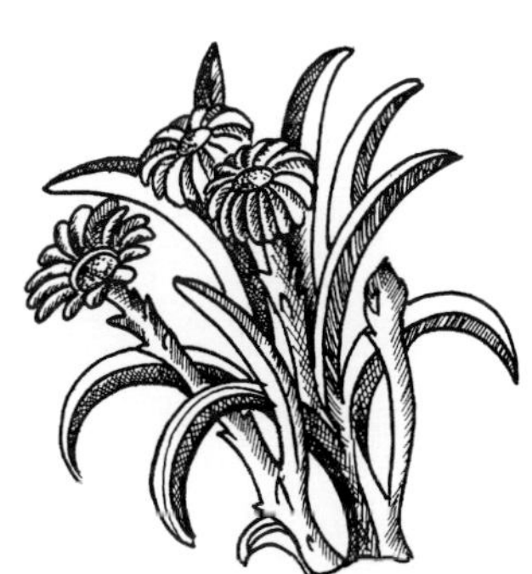

ASHFORD DISTRIBUTORS

Ashford products are available from craft shops around the world. For the name of your nearest stockist contact your national distributor.

NEW ZEALAND:
Ashford Handicrafts Limited
PO Box 474, Ashburton
Tel: (64-3) 308 9087 Fax: (64-3) 308 8664
E-mail: sales@ashford.co.nz
http://www.ashford.co.nz

AUSTRALIA:
Ashford Australia Pty Limited
Travellers Rest, Snowy Mountains Highway
Cooma, NSW 2630
Tel: (61-2) 64 524 422
Fax: (61-2) 64 524 523

AUSTRIA:
Wohnbauladen Alles Zum Gesunden Bauen
und Wohnen
Ing Volkmar Baurecker
Goethestrasse 38, A-4020 Linz
Tel: (0732) 60 22 44 0
Fax: (0732) 60 22 44 19

CANADA:
Treenway Crafts Limited
725 Caledonia Avenue
Victoria, British Columbia V8T 1E4
Tel: (250) 383 1661
Fax: (250) 383 0543

DENMARK:
Elsa Krogh
'Hevil', Havndalvej 40
9550 Mariager
Tel: (+45) 98 54 22 53
Fax: (+45) 98 54 22 53

FINLAND:
Toijalan Kaide KY, PL 25
Haittilantie 4, 37801 Toijala
Tel: (+358 3) 542 1095
Fax: (+358 3) 542 1001

FRANCE:
Ets P. Marie Saint Germain
9, rue du Capitaine
Flayelle 88203
Remiremont, Cedex
Tel: 33 3 29 23 00 48
Fax: 33 3 29 23 20 70

GERMANY:
Friedrich Traub KG
Schorndorfer Strasse 18
D-73650 Winterbach
Tel: (07181) 70910
Fax: (07181) 709111

JAPAN:
Ocean Trading Co Limited
2F, Kyoto Toshiba Bldg
25 Hira-machi, Saiin
Ukyo-ku Kyoto
Tel: (075) 314 8720
Fax: (075) 325 2450

Mariya Handicrafts Limited
Kita-1, Nishi-3, Chuo-Ku
Sapporo 060
Tel: (81-11) 221 3307
Fax: (81-11) 232 0393

Sanyo Trading Company Limited
Sanyo Building, Togashira 2-42-14
Torideshi, Ibaraki 302
Tel: 0297 78 1000
Fax: 0297 78 5850

REPUBLIC OF KOREA:
LDH Hand Weaving Loom, Fine Corp Ltd
CPO Box 6718
Seoul
Tel: (02) 779 1894
Fax: (02) 755 1663

NORWAY:
Spinninger
Postboks 136
1361 Billingstad
Tel: 66 84 60 22
Fax: 66 84 60 22

SOUTH AFRICA:
Campbell Crafts and Marketing
Rolfes House
6 Dorman Street, Gardens 8001
Cape Town

Tel: 021-233287
Fax: 021-221938

SWEDEN:
Gudruns Ullbod
Ulunda
745 91 Enkoping
Tel: (0171) 399 95
Fax: (0171) 399 96

SWTIZERLAND:
Spycher-Handwerk
Gradel, Bach, 4953 Schwarzenbach
b. Huttwil
Tel: (0629) 62 1152
Fax: (0629) 62 1160

TAIWAN:
Founder Tek Int'l Co Limited
7 Fl.,177, Sec 4, Chung Hsiao East Road
Taipei, ROC
Tel: (886-2) 781 1699/741 9007
Fax: (886-2) 751 2521

UNITED KINGDOM:
Haldanes Craft and Tools Limited
Gateside, Strathmiglo
Fife KY14 7ST
Tel: (01337) 860767
Fax: (01337) 860507

UNITED STATES:
Crystal Palace Yarns
3006 San Pablo Avenue
Berkeley, CA 94702
Tel: (510) 548 9988
Fax: (510) 548 3453